A LIFE WELL LIVED

A Life Well Lived

A Legacy of Lessons from My Father

Roger Kay

Falconart Media LLC

Copyright © MMXX by Roger Kay

ISBN-13: 978-0-9740804-5-1
ISBN-10: 0-9740804-5-4

Library of Congress Control Number: 2020930933

Text set in Palatino with Lesson titles
in Chalkduster on QuarkXPress

Book and cover design by George Allez
Photos by the author with noted exceptions

Cover photo by Kevin Kothrade of the
hands of Allen and Damian Kothrade,
the son, grandson and great-grandson
of the author.

Printed and bound in the USA

1 3 5 7 9 10 8 6 4 2

www.rogerkay.com

The falcon colophon and Falconart
are the copyrighted imprint of Falconart Media, LLC.
All rights reserved

Table of Contents

Prologue

Preface

Lesson One — The Rock River Monster Walleye
Be as enthusiastic about responsibility as you are about play

Lesson Two — Deer Lake Hideaway
The cost of privacy is responsibility

Lesson Three — Jeepers Creepers
Violating a trust always has consequences

Lesson Four — Running With the Big Dogs
Funny depends on which side of the fence you're on

Lesson Five — Deadman's Hill
I am my brother's keeper, and he, mine

Lesson Six — Hot Hand, Cool Head
Danger not only lurks, it grabs

Lesson Seven — Walking on Eggs
Women never say what they mean

Lesson Eight — One and Done
Womanhood has the right to civility

Lesson Nine — Provo Promises
Real men own up even if they're women

Lesson Ten — Better Living Through Chemistry
Fear does not make cowards

Lesson Eleven — Rattling Roofs
Anger will always cloud judgement

Lesson Twelve — Fountain City Bluff
Punishment should fit the crime

Lesson Thirteen — Sad Sacks
Don't assume you know people

Lesson Fourteen — Haymaker, Hero Maker
Loyalty is manliness

LESSON FIFTEEN — Devil and the Deep Blue
It's not always clear cut

LESSON SIXTEEN — Fish or Cut Bait
Stand your ground, but know it first

LESSON SEVENTEEN — Cousin Cousine
There is a big picture and it's not sex

LESSON EIGHTEEN — Bear in Mind
Keep both eyes open

LESSON NINETEEN — Moose-taken Identity
Life won't happen the way you expect

LESSON TWENTY — My Momentous Midnight Ride
Good deeds DO go unpunished

LESSON TWENTY-ONE — Pleasing the Old Man
Think bigger than you think you can do

LESSON TWENTY-TWO — Planning Ahead

EPILOGUE

"So soon old, so late smart."

~~ Anna Grahek, *my grandmother*

Prologue

The long driveway I came to know so well over the years, where Ma and Pa lived in their retirement lake home.

Knowing oneself is downright scary . . .

MY FATHER lies shrunken beneath the ghost-like sheets. Until this cold predawn November morning, he has always been a large man, perhaps larger in my mind than in reality, but nevertheless a strapping six foot three. With a laconic grin that would put Gary Cooper to shame, he has been the tower of strength and the epitome of manhood for the many decades of my life, and in fact, for our entire family as well. My only sibling, a brother seven years younger and as diametrically different from me as siblings can be, would relate to you the same hero worship stories as I will about the superman now weakly clutching my hand as I walk beside the wobble-wheeled gurney. The tiled corridor is barren and hollow but short, and it will soon end, at least for me, a mere fifty feet ahead at the double doors forbidding entry to anyone but cardiac team members.

That he is frightened is obvious to anyone who might look at the gaunt face, the listless gray hair. Why is it I never noticed before this morning the gray hair is not the lustrous brown I had assumed would never change? The look of fear, too, I see anew. It is a look I have never seen on this man. Fear is not a word that I associate with my father.

And I know well the face of fear. It has personally shown itself to me many times, in many places around the world, forever the same, yet always distinct. But the fear in my father's eyes, on his face, is not that fear of which I am painfully familiar. No, this fear is not for himself, but rather, it is reserved for my mother, the tiny silver-haired woman who walks beside me down this echoing chamber. His voice, a mere whisper, just as it has been for many years now, seems disembodied from the man I know, as though it were not he on this gurney, not he taking this journey. The urgent whisper implores me to come closer. And as I bend over close to his face, for the twentieth time in the last 30 minutes he pleads, "If something goes wrong, take care of your mother . . . promise me . . . " And I, of course, am flip, smiling, and confident . . . and terrified. As the elder son, the mantle of family leadership must fall on me.

  Six weeks earlier I had left my comfortable old trawler in Marina del Rey and come back to the family homestead on the shore of an azure blue lake deep in the north woods of Wisconsin. I had been through a bad patch and needed to recharge batteries by drawing energy from that deep well of family, of kinship. My mother, in spite of her arthritis and rheumatism, clucked happily as the elder son spent time sitting at the kitchen table watching the lake and slowly drawing sustenance from the air as if by osmosis. Too engrossed in my own problems, I gave only cursory notice to my folks. After all, they are always there. Always have been, always will be.

Prologue

When my mother suggested I might help my father remove a few trees that were too close to the house before I left to return to my sea-going home in California, I readily agreed. Since my parents would spend the long winter in Florida, the thought of a snow-laden branch falling on the roof and damaging her lakeside minicastle would prey on her mind the entire winter. Taking down a few trees was a small favor, particularly in light of the fact that Pa and I had, over the years, cut down thousands of trees for pulp, lumber, and income. My father decided to drop these into a narrow ten foot alleyway between the house and the woodshed, and I had no qualms about his ability to thread that needle with the four trees. It would be a matter of honor for my father to drop the tree exactly where he said it would fall. And he has rarely missed by more than a foot. My mother, of course, would look worried, chide my father to be careful and he would, just as he has done for all of their sixty years together, ignore her concerns about his work prowess. She is a woman. She does not understand about man's work. It is not her business. I know he thinks these thoughts; thus, not surprisingly, so do I. For him, a product of a world different from my own, self-sufficiency and the clear delineation of gender expectations is simply the way of his life. Would that it were as clear cut for me.

The mechanics of taking down the trees goes as expected, all four falling exactly on the proscribed arc predicted by my father's long arm. As we begin the limbing process and cleanup with the chainsaws, for the first time I sense the speed with which my father is working. Slow. Not his style. He has worked hard all his life whether it is puddling cement on a driveway, carrying people out of burning buildings, or clearing brush after felling a few trees. He is not a man to work slow.

His pace bothers me. And is he out of breath? For the first time in five days I actually look at my father. I am appalled at his visage. He is old. Oh, I know he is 78, but he's never been OLD before. His face is pale and he stoops. He moves slowly and with obvious pain. His gnarled fingers, distorted by myriad injuries over the hard years of his working life, seem unable to grasp the chain saw trigger with authority. I do not recognize this man.

I think to myself about how incredibly self-centered I have been for these past days. I help as best I can, anticipating small chores before he need do them, as we pile and clean up the fallen trees. A neat stack of brush, and an even stack of firewood has been added as fuel for those fall evenings that require some warmth before they leave for Florida. But I cannot find my father. Certainly, he is right there with us at the dinner table in front of the windows overlooking the lake, occupying the same chair he always has, but I do not see my father. I see a man old. Old and tired. It is a scene now etched within my ken.

It does haunt me during my return flight to LA and the land of tight faces and tighter psyches. I left my boat feeling pain, and returned healthy, just as I have done many times in my life. It is the magic of family and belonging. When I hear horror stories of families gone sour, or even simply gone, I wonder how others heal themselves. How do they fix the hurts of daily life? From whence does their life-balm come? It sets me once again to appreciating my parents, my family, and my father. And yet, although I know myself to be cured for a time, there is that small seed of doubt loitering about in the darker recesses of my mind. I have over the past four or five years paid lip service to preparing myself for the inevitable. But that man at our dinner table back in Wisconsin was a man ready to give over the mantle. And it scared me. And it reminded me harshly of my personal predilection to procrastination. I would need to seriously give thought to life without one or both of my parents.

    I convince myself that it will be a priority . . . as soon as I finish a play I'm writing. And I immerse myself once again in daily tribulations as effectively as if I were hibernating. I do not answer phones. I either let them ring or I let the computer chips talk for me, answer for me. So when I finally review my messages, there is a message from my mother, which is not unusual. She asks me to call. Also not unusual because I don't call nearly as often as I ought. I finish the scene I'm working on and fall into the bunk weary and decide to call in the morning. It is Sunday evening. Her call must have come either late Saturday or early Sunday. Regardless, I call her Monday early and she calmly says that Pa had a heart attack on Saturday. And I get one call, with no information? How is he, where is he and all of the other immediately necessary questions regurgitate in reflexive guilty reaction. She assures me it was quite minor and in fact he is going to come home today or tomorrow. What? What did the angiogram say? She doesn't think he's had one of those. . . . What did the doctors say about heart muscle damage? Very little damage she thinks.

My folks live in a tiny resort town a hundred miles from any large medical center and now I am not just worried, but extremely concerned. How could anybody send a heart attack victim home without testing for blockage, valve, or muscle damage? I remain calm, but tell Mom not to worry, that I will be back home as soon as I can get a flight. She protests and says Father also says to stay put and not worry. Fine, I say, as soon as I hang up, I am already on the line to the airlines. Next call is to the doctor in charge of my father. In no uncertain terms I tell her he needs to have a complete workup. She of course informs me that she has already made arrangements with the cardiac center in Duluth for my father's tests. She says she has not told him yet because he is not the world's greatest patient, demanding to leave her clinic before she even got to examine him, but promising to return Monday for her results. The two of us agree that he will be sent directly via ambulance to the heart center in Duluth a hundred miles away. No stops at home for him because he'll surely find a way to put off the tests given the least opportunity. Her accurate appraisal of my father's character sustains me somewhat. She must have a good handle on him, I think to myself. On Monday he is transported to the cardiac

Prologue

center as promised by the doctor. Tests will commence early on Tuesday.

Because acquiring money is not one of my strengths, I must often rely on previous accumulations of frequent flier miles to do my traveling. Anyone who has plumbed the depths of any of the various redemption programs offered by the airlines knows that getting a quick, free flight is an oxymoron. But I have a few days before tests on him will be available, so I persevere and am able to arrange a convoluted but free flight plan on the coming Friday that will take me through three or four airports but ultimately drop me off a mere 120 miles from my folks' home. Luckily I have a good friend in that city and can borrow a car for a few days. The arrangements are set and I relax as best I can, given my internal guilt about having just been home and concerned only with my own darkness.

The tests go easily on Tuesday with my father in good spirits but I can tell from his hesitation he is unsure as to what is being done or even as to what his specific malady might be. His answers to my questions are vague and not to my liking, plus my attempts to reach his cardiologist are futile. I can understand a doctor's propensity for packing the day, but I want to know the results as badly as do my folks.

It is hard for me to separate the fear for his condition and the selfish fear for my condition if he were to leave me. Particularly with much unsaid between us. Actually, mostly unsaid on my part, since it is I who have never properly thanked him for being the hero to me he has always been. I often tell others of his idolhood, and I write about it in my stories because his presence shapes my life in so many ways. But yet . . . I have never said it to his face. And it needs to be said while I can look into his eyes, so that he will see the depth of my gratitude. One of my most cherished hopes is that my own son might grow to feel even one-half as good about me as I do about my father. I know these needs are my personal needs, but they nevertheless would loom large if I should fail to carry out the simple task of expressing my gratitude. It is not as though this were a recent revelation to me. I have felt this bond since I turned 18. Some thirty-odd years later I have yet to come to grips with acknowledging my love, my gratitude, my life, to this man. Surely, I believed, I had so much more time.

It is Wednesday and for the first time in my entire life my traveling bag is packed and waiting two days prior to departure. I have always thrown things in a bag the morning of the flight even if it were a long overseas trip. I do not know where my propensity for procrastination comes from. Neither of my folks has so obvious a fault. Nor does my brother. Nor my son. I am the family deviant, borne out by my unconventional decisions in life. And in spite of much evidence to my ongoing careless decision making, neither Pa nor Ma has ever been judgmental. Their comment today is the same as the one I heard at age 18 when I announced I would not go back to medical school although we had talked about and planned for it since I was the eight-year-old wunderkind. No screaming and no yelling, but instead a simple, "you have to live your own life" was the only comment uttered, even though I know the disappointment nearly broke their hearts. Private grief, and private joy. Family hallmarks. And yet, never has there been any question of support, or loyalty, or love. Could one ask for better family values? I think not.

Broken out of my reverie by my mother's latest call, I listen to her explanations of the test results. The comments make no sense to me and I know I need to speak to the cardiologist directly. My father thinks he can come home in spite of some "blockage" and I am stern with Ma. Who said he could leave? What percentage of blockage? Why doesn't the doctor call me back? I hang up and call my father directly, so I can judge for myself his state of mind. He sounds better but still tired, and sure enough, he does think he is going to go home. I am not pleased with this turn of events. And once again, I cannot help but wonder if it is my own fear that permeates my thinking, refusing to recognize the true situation a long two thousand miles and a longer 48 hours away.

When I finally get through to the cardiologist, he gives me the facts. Although a nearly complete blockage of a major artery has caused an angina attack, through a fluke of nature, some slight anomaly in my father's heart, blood flowed through a sort of "back door" that prevented his immediate death and in fact caused the attack to be quite minor. The cardiologist says he can't understand it and surely my father should be dead or at least contending with major muscle tissue damage. Instead, they propose to do three or four bypasses and expect him to not only recover but be much improved over his pre-attack condition. The doctor does mention that my father wishes to check himself out and go home. I call my father and we settle the issue at once. He will have the bypass operation.

    And so, as the wobble-wheeled gurney carrying my life disappears through the dreaded double doors, and those doors ominously swing shut, I am left in the hall with my mother and my brother while the reverberating echo of our footsteps mocks my false bravado. With palpable fear etched on my own heart, I put my arms around Ma and we walk to the special cardiac waiting room. I know the tears in my eyes are matched by those of Ma and Tom, my kid brother, but my own fears crowd out concerns about the two of them. Why does this dark trait of egoism afflict me and me alone in our family? No one else in the family shows this flaw. Why could I not be more like my father instead of the wayward black sheep that I am?

    I cannot recall a single detail of the waiting room. My eyes will not focus on the words in the magazine, the pictures on the wall, not even my mother's face. My breathing is labored and erratic as I stare off into the void of an empty life without Pa. That everyone goes through similar emotions at the death of a loved one, I have no doubt, but I honestly had not expected the loss to immobilize my thought process to this extent. I always considered myself above such plebian human responses. Whenever I hurt, I could simply go home, even if only in my mind, and there I would find the salve to soothe the pain, heal the wound. Now where could I go? Where would the healing power come from? Being the loner these many years, I would now be expected to once again take responsibility. Responsibility . . . for myself, my mother, my family. The frightening true meaning of fatherhood stands out in sharp relief. Honor, duty, family.

As if a bystander, I watch my growing fear tearing away the sheaves of the carefully constructed straw house image of myself as a man. Ripping and tearing away to reveal a pale and impotent reflection of my father. Where now was his courage and bravery that was supposedly mine by genetic right? Why could I not stand to this, as I had against those many physical dangers to my being? Where **now** those vaunted ice-filled veins so many have accused me of? If not the rock I had patterned myself after, who was I? Who could I be? Worse, **could** I be?

I cannot remember the surgeon coming to tell us my father was fine, that everything had gone better than he had hoped. I can barely remember my father looking a startling 15 years younger only hours after the surgery. My brother told me later that he was so frightened he could not understand how I could have remained so calm and caring to our mother and reassuring to him. I managed only a blank stare at him. Surely, he was saying this to be

Roger Kay

kind to me and my shattered self image. But he persisted. Who was he talking about? I do not know. I do know, however, if I *had* acted as he says I did, that person was not me. It could only have been one person. It could only have been Pa . . . looking after us, just as he always has, just as he always will.

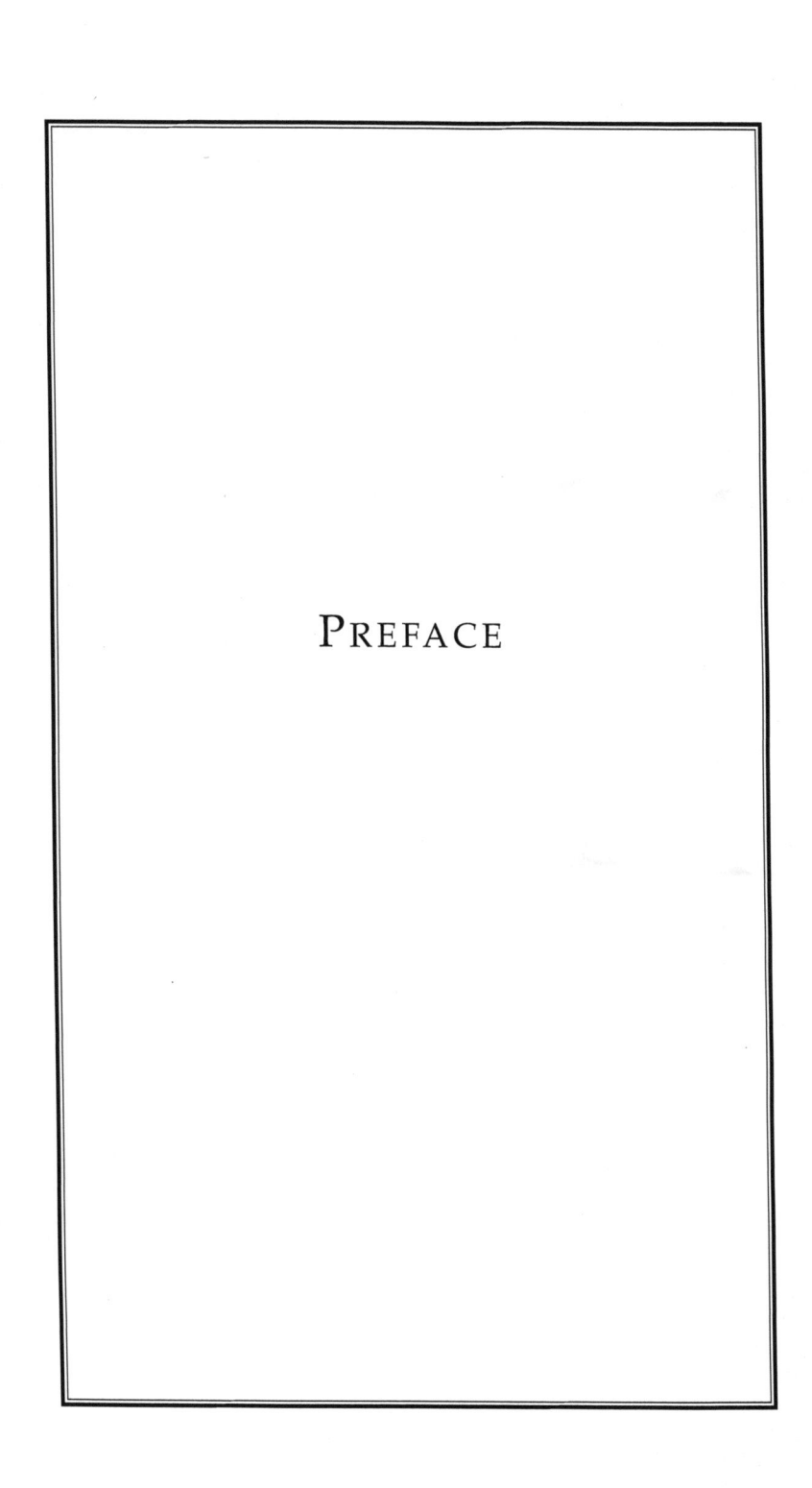

Preface

Ma and Pa on their wedding day

Preface

WHEN I BEGAN WRITING THIS, both of my parents were in their late seventies, married for nearly sixty years and both still filled with passion for life and the health to enjoy it. When I told my mother I was contemplating writing down my memories as a youth about Pa and the things he taught me, I also mentioned that perhaps she might help me with a few insights of her own. After all, she knew this man better than he knew himself. Her response surprised me. She said, "If you think you truly know every part of another human being, either that person isn't worth knowing or you are a fool. Thank God I am afflicted with neither problem."

Such wisdom has been forthcoming whenever I have had the good sense to ask either of them for advice. In truth, this is about both my parents, because they have always been as one to me. Unfortunately, I am my father's son and carry forward some of those anachronistic European ideas of machismo, heroes, and male as protector of the fairer and gentler sex. I know intellectually that "the who" and "the why" of my father is due in no small part to my mother who is, without question, the most wonderful woman in the world.

Later in the process, I realized that the man I was writing about, just as my mother had predicted, remained a mystery to me in a myriad of ways. When I recognized that relating his story was actually telling mine, it was an epiphany. My memories mirror him and his actions for the most part, but the true meaning of these actions is to be found in their reflection within me. I have no doubt I did not enter into his conscious thoughts during these related encounters, rather he, simply going about his own life, expected me to gather the threads of my own coping skills through osmosis or trial and error, as surely he must have done. That these moments are so vivid to me only confirms my opinion that they were as he expected them to be, my guideposts, my trail-markers along the pathways of my unfolding life.

The quiet and intense wisdom of my father and mother confronts me nearly every day of living, but the initial images, those moments of epiphany and clear sight, stand out as a true sea change on the surface of my existence. I need to further clarify that these moments are of my personal remembering, not to be confused with my father's testimony, which, even were he to offer it, would flatly deny and soundly scoff at the least hint of heroism. But the heroism was there then, and remains today for not only me, but also for my brother, and the many others who came into contact with my father over the years.

Too often in our society we hear of an unhappy childhood blamed on parents. I blame my happiness in life on my parents. I would like to be able to report that I have kept to the course set by my parents, but, like most of us, I have strayed off course at times, not because of their failure, but because of my own lack of ability to see clearly in the smoggy haze of hectic living. Nevertheless, I am cheered by one thought in particular . . . should my own child think half as much of me as I think of my parents, my life will have been a success. Did I come to know Pa through my reflections? As usual, my mother was correct, but I've come to grips with not knowing Pa completely. However, I do know one thing completely and truly — both that part of Pa that I do know, AND that part I do not, I will forever idolize.

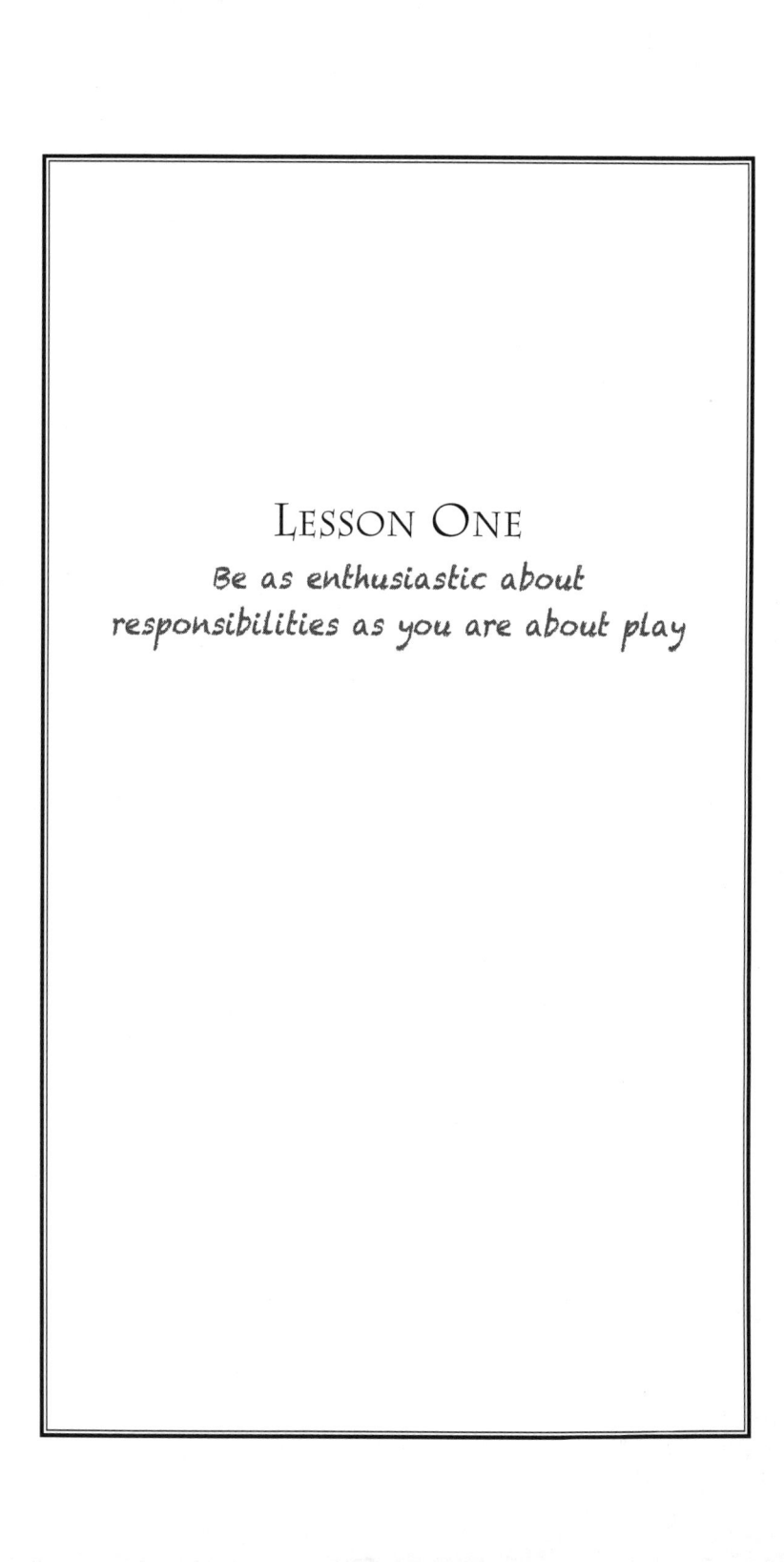

Lesson One
Be as enthusiastic about responsibilities as you are about play

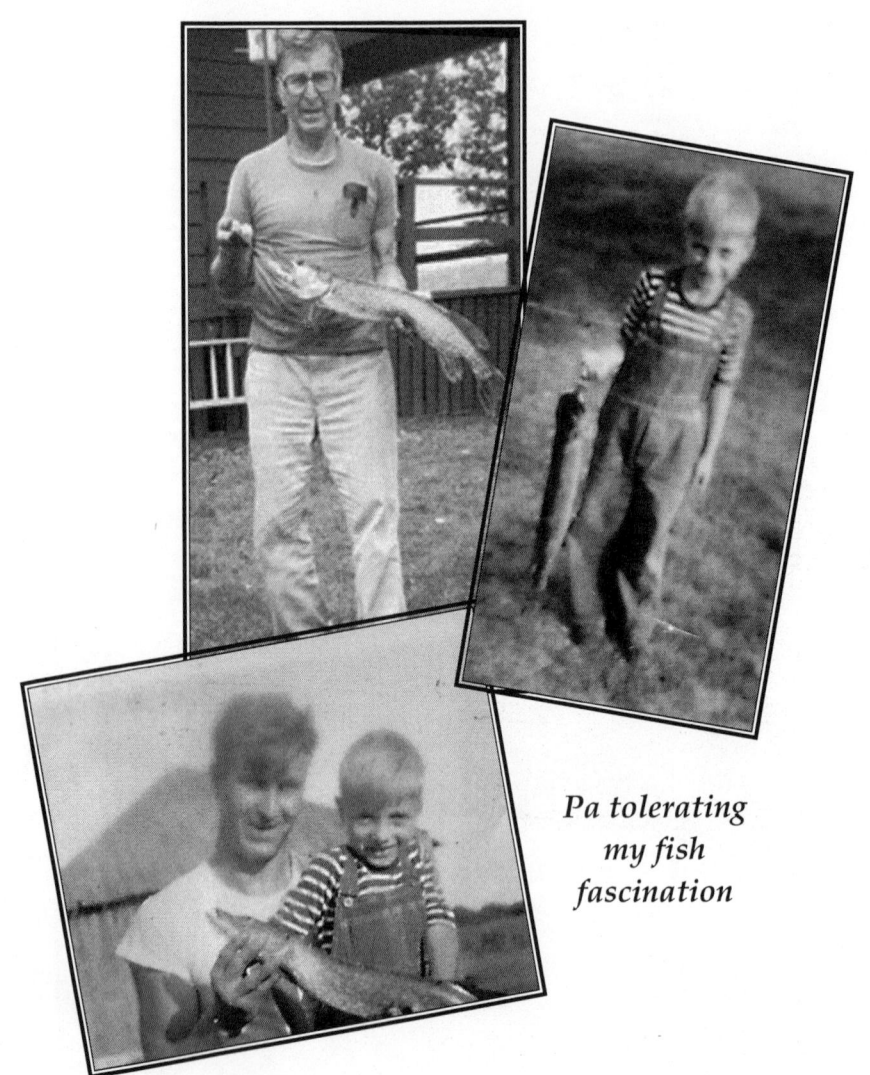

Pa tolerating my fish fascination

The Rock River Monster Walleye

For a period of two or three years before my tenth birthday, one event, or perhaps more correctly, one activity captured my imagination like no other, with the exception of staying awake to see Santa. I longed for the swift passage of January, February, March, and finally April. Not that I didn't enjoy the winter months, mind you, because the ice skating, sledding, and snow fort building were crucial skills for a young boy to master and I took to them with great zeal. No, rather the longing occurred in those short moments just before sleep, when a rainbow of stars burst behind my eyelids and signaled the end of another exciting day. It was in those brief pregnant moments that my mind flashed forward to the coming of spring, more specifically the official opening of the walleye season on the Rock River.

I cannot fathom at this time what it was that made me so enamored of the activity of spring fishing on that river. My memories are not in the least clouded about any of the two or three times each spring Pa would take me to the same place and we would engage in manly talk and pit our strength and cunning against that of the Monster Walleyed Pike who hid in the frigid fast flowing depths of the Rock River, awaiting only the right moment to grab my bait and yank me into his swirling milieu. My father's constant admonition to keep well away from the slippery river bank only added to the danger in our adventure.

When the sky no longer held the promise of fresh snow, and the remnants of my last snow fort were no more than black-speckled mounds of remelted snow, I would listen carefully at the breakfast table for those important words from my father's mouth, carefully hidden though it might be behind the morning newspaper. "Hmm, walleye season opens this week." That was my signal to engage in my trait of hectoring and badgering for what I desired that would later in life cause me substantial grief. But parents must accept a certain amount of this behavior to allow the child to develop a sense of anticipation to offset the practicing of patience. Instant gratification remains to this day a concept stillborn in our family. Patience and anticipation were opposites to be balanced and controlled, one in each hand, so the value of each could be judged and used in future endeavors.

As the tension rose to when the exact day might occur, that one day with the weather warm enough, school out, and Pa off duty from his job as a fireman, I was rarely able to contain my enthusiasm. Nearly every evening I would sneak downstairs into the basement, gently slide the rusty old green tackle box off the top workbench shelf, and quietly as I could manage, unsnap the clasps. As each tier of nooks and crannies successively revealed itself, my eyes would select the evening's project. With tens of strangely shaped and colorfully painted lures beckoning to me, I passed them all, and went directly to the only piece of tackle we would need for the Rock River Monster Walleye . . . the famous Wolf River Rig. Why it was named the Wolf River Rig although we would only use it to fish on the Rock River, I never thought to inquire. I did know that the "Wolf" was another fishing river, farther up in the wilds of "the North Country." My own river, the Rock, was as large a river as my imagination could carry.

    The "rig," as my father called it, was a simple swivel device connected to the end of the main fishing line with two 16-inch arms, one holding a three ounce weight at its end, and the other arm with the gleaming No. 13 snelled fishhook that could put your eye out in a flash of carelessness or embed itself in your hand, not to be recovered without excruciating pain. A simple device, it allowed the sinker to drop toward the bottom in the swift spring current, while the hook with a live lip-impaled minnow would be free to wiggle and waggle unfettered in the middle of the Rock's raging spring runoff current and tantalize Mister Monster Walleye.

    Carefully polishing the hooks and the swivels, I would replace them as I found them and sneak back upstairs secure in the knowledge that I had fully prepared the weapons of our assault. And on that long awaited morning itself, cereal, toast, or any other item placed in front of me intended as a speed bump, would simply be inhaled. Pa would take forever to finish one measly cup of black coffee. Still dark, we would load the old Buick with the fishing gear and the sandwiches Ma had made for our lunch. Leaving home in the damp dark before dawn was the exclamation mark of my early life, because it only happened on momentous occasions, like fishing trips, vacations, or going up to my Uncle's dairy farm for a few days. All those events being important and exciting life moments for a ten-year-old.

    I'm sure sunrise was beautiful but during all the times Pa and I went to the Rock, I always fell asleep under the gentle sway and hypnotic hum of our fat Buick, and only awakened as we pulled in at the bait store to buy the minnows. Still rubbing the sand of sleep from my eyes, I would follow Pa into the dank interior of the bait shop. Tanks of all sizes, bubbling, spritzing, and hissing menacingly, each with its own specific sized denizen, loomed nose high around me like miniature rivers with miniature monsters of the deep waiting their chance to tempt real monsters. At each outing I was amazed at the baitman's speed and ability to count out the three dozen minnows Pa always bought. While he paid, I would stare down into the bait bucket and count as quickly as I might, but never getting beyond five before they became hopelessly confused with their brethren. It was many years before I realized the baitman couldn't count to thirty-six that fast either, but for a long time, he remained in my mind, a man of inexplicable talent and skill.

    With the pale yellow spring sun climbing into the morning sky, dew sparkled on the tiny new leaves of the oaks and elms dotting the rolling hills. The hills themselves were painted with a shimmering green of spring grasses, and I could always sense when we were close to our epic battleground. Would this be the day I caught the Monster, or would he win the battle and pull me into his river before Pa could grab my coat and save me? Anxious but determined, I prepared myself as we pulled off the highway thirty or forty yards and parked. With the engine off, the sudden quiet within the old Buick was disconcerting, but as I opened my door, the distant soft roar of the Rock River grabbed my attention. It was only another twenty or thirty yards along a path surely trod by Chippewas, Oneidas, and Potawatomies before me, down to the river itself. With banks twice as high as me, the muted roar would not sound it's full fury until we stood right next to the icy churning waters.

    I would remember the rest of the day only in terms of small incidents: Pa allowing me to be the first to reach into the icy minnow bucket to grasp the wily minnow; Pa patiently resetting my pole because I would need to lift it every 60 or 70 seconds to see if the minnow was still wagging his tail; Pa helping me remove a nonmonster walleye off the hook: And most often, Pa smiling at me when, for the thousandth time I would ask him if our "monster" was still lurking near our dangling hooks. Riding home with fish or riding home skunked, it made no difference, for the day was always a great adventure. An adventure to be related to a mother who listened attentively but who, as even I could sense, had no interest in the manly sport of stalking the "monster" of the Rock River.

It was fully thirty years later when, during an evening reminiscing with my mother about Pa, I mentioned how the two of us had not been fishing since I was a boy. "Not surprising," she said, "since your father always hated fishing."

"What?" I cried, "he loved those days we spent on the Rock fishing for walleyes!"

"Oh don't be silly," she said, "He only went because you got so excited about it every spring."

All those years and I never suspected that our "Rock River monster expeditions" were solely for my benefit. I truly believed he looked forward to them as much as me. Treating me, a small boy filled with the excitement of anticipation, to a rarified view from that narrow window that looks forward into adulthood. Pa generously gave me a brief but precious glimpse of one more potential path leading to my future. I think back now on the myriad of incidents in which I was exposed to new experiences because of a commitment to his responsibility to provide me the tools to design my own life. And he always did so with a smile on his face. And so it was that I learned (albeit quite late) to be as enthusiastic about responsibility as I was about play.

Lesson Two
The cost of privacy is responsibility

The first of many significant piers in my life

Deer Lake Hideaway

ONCE EVERY SUMMER until well into my early teens, our family took a full week's vacation up north to what my folks called "God's Country." The first few years it merely meant a long, long drive peppered with my questions . . . i.e. "are we there yet?" By the time I was twelve, the week was the summer's high point. Pa and Ma would sit at the kitchen table for a couple of hours discussing and deciding where and which lake would be this summer's "lake week." Meanwhile my brother Tom and I would try to locate the chosen lake on one of the myriads of road maps that were scattered about the kitchen table. Once that decision was made it remained only to decide if we would share the week on our Deer Lake hideaway with any cousins. My mother had eight sisters and so a plethora of cousins were available for companionship and this particular year we arranged to rent two adjacent cabins with an aunt and uncle whose two daughters matched the ages of my brother and myself, five and twelve.

    The interminable wait for the golden August week eventually ended and we caravanned the two cars, our lumbering Buick and their sleek new Nash, three hundred miles north to the small private lake that had only our two summer cabins on its shores. A true hideaway fit even for Al Capone! My one memory of the long car ride was a brief exchange between Ma and Pa after leaving home a little later than we had planned.

"Hope we get there before dark," Ma offered, as Pa chuckled and said it didn't matter much because we'd have a full moon for a couple of days and "we probably wouldn't even need headlights under that big bright moon."

Seven hours later, while our folks unloaded the cars and opened up the cabins, we four kids ran willy-nilly down the gentle hillside slope to the shore of Deer Lake and its one pier. The magical view of the small private lake and the two small rowboats on each side of the wooden pier promised the four of us an entire week of adventuring. Best news of all was that this was the first year Tom and our younger cousin knew how to swim and so we would be allowed to take out the boats without adults aboard. The "kids only" private boat excursions beckoned like a blazing beacon as we stood transfixed, looking over our new unexplored domain.

Called back to the cabins, we had real decisions to make; where did we want our tents set up? Girls in one and Tom and I in the other, this was not an easy decision. We wanted the tents close to each other but not so close that we would both not have privacy but more important, it had to be far enough away from our parents and their two cabins. If the weather stayed summer-like, we'd sleep out in our tents every night exploring the new experience of privacy from adult supervision. Stay up as late as we liked every night! Nobody yelling at us from downstairs to "turn out the lights and quiet down!" How could life be any better for us lucky preteens?

Just as Pa had predicted, that night was as bright as daylight with a huge moon hanging above the trees and even showing as a hazy glow through our old canvas tents. Until well after midnight, we laughed, told horror stories, made scary faces with our flashlights, but always came back to the same theme . . . what would be the first things we'd explore in the morning? And of course, they all involved taking out the rowboats and exploring the lake without our parents!

Normally my choice for summer mornings was to let them pass while I slept. This summer morning, however, could not be wasted as all four of us were up before the birds could sing us awake. Given explicit warnings that although we could sleep for as long as we wished, breakfast would be served only once and only when our moms rang the convenient outdoor bell. Miss the call and we'd have to wait for lunch. We did not venture too far from our tents as much as we would have liked to explore for fear we would not hear the bell. At the rate adrenalin was coursing through our veins, we desperately needed the fuel breakfast would provide.

It was a race between the cousins to see who could finish breakfast and race to the boats first. We did not win that race because my pokey brother Tom was a picky eater and even with the boats eagerly awaiting our arrival he still picked at his cereal and toast while I fumed. In sixty years, that has not changed. When we finally ran down the hill to the boats, we never noticed our parents putting out the lawn chairs and settling in with steaming coffee cups for a well-earned respite from jabbering kids. Of course, we paid no attention to the shouts of "be careful" as we dashed off into our new, personal wilderness. We did observe the rules so although we all were decent swimmers, we were not allowed to get in the boats without wearing our lifejackets. It was a small price to pay for the privacy of exploring without adults!

The morning passed with the discovery of turtles, lily pads, frogs and jumping fish and then the lunch bell sounded across the lake and both boats rowed the race to shore and lunch. We won that one, somewhat lessening the sting of having lost the first race down to the boats this morning. By late afternoon we had spent nearly the entire day on the hard rowboat seats and did not care about comfort. As both boats met up again midlake and rowed at a more leisurely pace back to shore, Tom asked if the moon was going to be as bright as it was last night. My older cousin Carol and I answered simultaneously that it would be bright for a couple of more nights yet. Then Tom dropped the bombshell.

"We should go out for midnight boat rides," he blurted. Using the boats after dark was strictly forbidden unless one of our parents was with us in the boat. Cousin Carol quickly said, "We can't take the boats out after dark."

"Who would know?" Tom said. "We don't use the motor and we could be quiet with the oars."

During this interlude I said nothing, but the wheels were turning. Yes, it was forbidden, but Tom was right; it could be done very quietly. We had perfected the technique of quiet rowing while sneaking up on basking turtles. If a turtle couldn't hear us, certainly sleeping parents a hundred yards away in a cabin wouldn't hear us! And the idea of being in the middle of the lake under a brilliant bright moon was exciting to me. A new dangerous adventure about which I could brag to my buddies back home! The idea was extremely appealing. That's when I made the decision. "OK," I said loudly, "we'll do it tonight. At midnight. Are you both in as well?" I inquired of my cousins. They were hesitant. None of us had much experience in defying what we thought to be very strict parents. But I could tell that Carol was as intrigued as I was because her face gave her away. She was smiling. And then she shook her head and plainly said, "Yes, let's do it."

"Wow, wow, wow," Tom laughed, "I was just kidding. I didn't think we could really do it."

With this secret weighing heavily on all four of us, we were strangely subdued throughout supper and the marshmallow s'mores extravaganza around the campfire as well. Back in out tents we awaited the midnight hour and I began to re-examine my decision-making process. Yes, I wanted this new and dangerous adventure. Wait — dangerous? Was it safe? We'd be wearing our lifejackets, so yes, it would be safe. What could go wrong? And besides, the moon was even brighter than it was last night. Nevertheless, there was that tiny niggling doubt in the back of my mind.

    We sneakily made our way down to the pier, purposely not using our flashlights lest we were spotted by one of our parents. We had decided we would wait for at least half an hour after all the lights went out in the cabins so we could be assured no one was awake. In spite of the bright moonlight, each of us stumbled repeatedly as we tried to be "Indian quiet" on our sojourn. We four stood on the pier for a few more seconds than we had thought. Perhaps the enormity of our transgression was beginning to seep into our consciousness. I poked my brother and whispered, "This was your idea. Get in the boat."

    He was reluctant but finally said, "We're all going in one boat, aren't we?"

    "Yes." Both Carol and I said.

    "So, get in, you Doofus," I challenged him.

    As Tom stepped into the boat, it moved away from the dock. His arms windmilling, he fell between the boat and the pier before I could grab hold of him.

    "Who tied up the boat wrong?" I rasped, as I jumped into the water to grab Tom. The water, shallow so close to the shore, only came up a little over my thighs but it would be up to Tom's chest ... IF he could stand. When I reached for him, I grabbed nothing! And it was dark! I could not see a thing next to the pier or under it. Worse, I did not think to use the flashlight hanging from my belt. Where was he? Did I not hear his splashing and whimpering because I was wildly flailing myself trying to grab anything I thought would be my brother? When I finally did grab his lifejacket, he was halfway underneath the pier coughing and sputtering. I hugged him first and then lifted him onto the pier where our cousins pulled him up. We quietly slunk back uphill to our tents without anyone saying a word. It would be several hours later, lying in bed recalling the events of the night, that I would remember that it was me who had not tied up the stern of the rowboat. Tom and I got up extra early in the morning, went down to the lake and splashed around to get our clothes wet so as to have an excuse for changing out of wet clothes before breakfast. The incident was never mentioned again by anyone as far as I knew.

    Fast forward perhaps twenty years. Me sitting with Ma at the kitchen table at their retirement home on Nelson Lake just outside of Hayward, Wisconsin. Coincidentally, not more than twenty miles from the infamous Deer Lake Hideaway. I asked Ma if she remembered that summer vacation at Deer Lake.

    "Do you mean the first time you nearly drowned your brother?"

    "WHAT?" I responded. "What do you remember about Deer Lake?"

    "Well let's see. I remembered you and your brother scaring the living daylights out of us when you decided to go boat riding at midnight," she replied with a smirk on her face.

    "When and how did you find out about it?. Did Tom or one of the cousins blab?"

    "Oh, for Heaven's sakes. We knew about it the minute you talked about it."

"But how did . . . ?"

"You, my son, who has sailed all over the world and been on boats since you were a kid, should have figured it out. Surely you know how far a voice carries over still water. Your father, me and your aunt and uncle were all sitting out on the lawn the afternoon you decided to be bad and we heard everything as though you were standing right in front of us."

"And you just let us go ahead with the plan? It could have been a lot worse. That night could have been disastrous," I said.

"Oh, your dad was pretty worried all right, especially if you had decided to take two boats. That's why we sat in the dark, him with his binoculars watching you every step of the way down the hill. Then he would have come roaring down there like thunder I'm sure. But when we could see it was just one boat, he knew we could get to you quickly with the other if it was necessary. Touch and go for a few minutes there I will admit, but it all worked out. All four of you looked pretty well chastised when you came back up to the tents. Your Pa felt strongly about letting you make your own mistakes and own up to your responsibilities. Yup, seemed like a lesson well learned we all thought. Best to let it go."

And so they did. For twenty odd years!
And Pa was right about something else. Privacy does come at a cost. And that cost is responsibility. A lesson I only wish I had learned that night. Sadly, as with many of his lessons, I was a little slow to catch on.

Lesson Three
*Violating a Trust
<u>Always</u> Has Consequences*

*Smart enough to shoot,
not smart enough to pull a haylifter*

Jeepers Creepers

Pa WAS OF THAT generation who felt it part of one's duty as a human being to help whomever asked for it. As my mother liked to say, "Your father would even help the devil if he asked." I believe Pa simply felt that it was wrong to not help someone who needed it whether or not he was asked. And my uncle who owned the small dairy farm in central Wisconsin was someone who often needed help because his three boys were at an age when they were often gone for periods of time — the army, new adventures, and bigger worlds. During those years, I turned twelve, a magical year for a boy on a small dairy farm in central Wisconsin. Twelve years of age represented watershed time, as one was legally granted two manly rights. Between the first, carrying my own gun while hunting, and the second, driving the farm tractor anywhere, it was the year of finally reaching my recognized manhood.

The first of these manly perks, carrying my own rifle or shotgun while we hunted the various seasons was just a refinement of previous outings. I had carried my own gun even when I was much younger, but it had to be in the presence of a supervising adult. One of our family of hunters, Pa or Uncle Roy, or Cousin

Bob or Cousin Dave or Cousin Rolly would always have to be in the vicinity acting as the responsible adult. Guns and gun safety were part and parcel of growing up on a farm in Wisconsin and I was lucky to have an entire family of superb role models when it came to guns and hunting. Other matters perhaps not so much, but guns were serious business in farm life and I grew up around them gaining a respect for the use and care of firearms.

But this was different. No longer did I have to badger any of the family to go rabbit or squirrel hunting. Pheasant and ducks and geese would certainly have a decidedly worse chance of survival now that I could venture out on my own whenever the mood struck me. I did not have to beg someone to take time out of a working day (EVERY day was a working day on a farm) to accompany me while I played hunter. Now, I could take a gun and go hunting on my own. No adult supervision needed! To a twelve-year-old that was heady stuff. I had already received the obligatory and constant safety and responsibility lecture from Pa and then Ma. But then from Uncle Roy as well. And then, Aunt Sophie. And of course, Cousin Bob. And finally, Cousin Dave. I would have had to listen to THE LECTURE a seventh time if the youngest of the farm cousins, Rolly, had been around, but luckily for me he was off working somewhere or in the Army at the time.

That first spring and summer of my free-fire, gun-toting, standing tall with a loaded lethal weapon was nirvana. I somehow believed boxes and boxes of ammunition would magically appear in the gun cabinet, just as my current dog Indee will stand and stare at her food bowl for hours if you let her, awaiting the magical appearance of food. Twelve gauge, 16 gauge in several pellet sizes, deer slugs and other shotgun shells, .22 and .408 and .30-06 and .30-30, even .44-40 rifle bullets all magically appeared on their proper shelves whenever I loaded up for the day. It never occurred to this 12-year-old man-child that ammunition cost money. Lots of money. And that was an item always in short supply on any small dairy farm. Food? Plenty. Clothes? Always something coming off of my Aunt's sewing machine. Building materials? Wood for the stoves? Plenty of trees around and tons of deadwood for fuel.

As the busy summer season for farm work approached, I overheard a short conversation between Pa and my Uncle Roy.

"You need any more gun ammunition?" asked Pa.

"The boy does go through it pretty fast," Uncle Roy replied.

"Yup, boys and guns. Knew it would be like this."

"Ain't no difference from my boys at that age," Roy stoically mumbled. "They get over it."

"Just want to make sure you have enough and don't want you paying for it, seeing as how it's him using it all up every week."

"Small price for all your help around here."

"Nonsense, I'll keep the cabinet supplied.

Besides, no better place for a young boy from the city to spread his wings a bit," Pa replied. "I figure I'm gettin' the best of the deal."

"Doubt it," chuckled my uncle.

That short exchange brought my profligate wild west lifestyle into a more focused perspective. I did not want to give up the adrenalin of shooting guns but deep down I knew none of our families had much money for extras. The entire family saved for nearly everything we bought and here I was throwing nickels, dimes, quarters and even dollars at tin cans on a fence post and the few wild game meals I was able to actually hit. The first beginnings of guilt crept into my head. That guilt, not just for this particular issue, but for a thousand other issues that would infect my mind for decades to come, (thank you Jesuits and a Jesuit education) caused me to seek the balm of redemption. This search for redemption on the farm just happened to coincide with the first haying season. And brought into play the second of my new manhood perks. Driving the tractor for real work.

We had a pair of 30 acre hayfields (large for our small farm) that produced two crops a summer and stored in our barns would last through the winter until spring. These two fields were bisected by the McCann trout stream. Although many fly fishermen stopped and asked to fish our stream, I personally never caught a fish out of that damn stream. It averaged between 10 and twenty feet wide with depths that could reach four or five feet but usually flowed with a frigid three foot current. It drained the two marshy hayfields and was bordered by saplings, high thorn bushes and too often by water moccasin snakes. It was a place I ventured seldom without my trusty .22 Remington to protect myself from death by snake bite.

    My plan for redemption was simple. I would offer to drive the Little Allis, our tractor, while we picked up the hay that had been cut the day before. Although we were not baling it like we would have for alfalfa, it still had to be stored in the barn hay lofts before any rain could cause mold while it still lay in the field. So the hay was cut with a ten foot flat scissor mower but needed then to be raked into collectable rows. To save time and fuel, the tractor would pull a side rake that produced one even row of mown hay, followed offset by a tall raking unit that would pick up the rows cleanly and lift them up and over into the hay wagon towed last in the parade of four vehicles..

    All together the three pieces of equipment behind the tractor stretched well over a hundred feet. Of course, modern equipment does all this in far more compact lengths, including baling and stacking bales on a wagon automatically, but we are talking small and impoverished dairy farming in the 1950s. When older folks refer to something being held together with baling wire, they were describing our little dairy farm. Literally, baling wire was used for every repair it seemed.

    My offer to be a real help did have a dual purpose. I would actually be helping with necessary work but I also got to drive the tractor. It had a motor and it pulled stuff! At age twelve, what could be more exciting if you could not drive a car? Since both fields were ready for harvesting my offer was met with some skepticism but the sheer number of hands with both Pa and myself joining Uncle Roy, Bob and Dave would make it a one day job instead of two. Saving an entire day of labor was a good thing during the "never long enough" summer season. I was in as driver of the tractor train because it was all straight lines, but mostly because it was the only job not requiring physical size and strength.

    The other labor saving device on the farm was a Korean War vintage jeep Cousin Bob had bought after the war and it was used as a shuttle vehicle during harvesting days. While one hay wagon was being loaded in the field, the previous full wagon was hitched to the jeep and towed back to the hay barn to be unloaded. This cycle was repeated four or five times a day while haying season was in operation.

    On the day that is engraved on my memory, I was being very helpful driving the tractor and the three pieces of equipment behind me while the other wagon was being driven to the barn by Cousins Bob and Dave. After the last run of the day, it was decided to take the train and move it to the hayfield across the McCann so we could get an early start in the morning. Pa had already left to help Roy with the repair job and Bob said he needed the tractor to get something out of the swampy marsh area and could Dave give him a hand? That left me. But without the tractor, the only towing vehicle was the jeep.

Bob looked at me and said, "You can drive the Jeep, right?"

Dave jumped right in and offered that it was just like the tractor with a clutch and a shift lever except there were three speeds instead of four. Now, at the age where boys can think of little else but driving a vehicle, ANY kind of motorized vehicle, a real Army Jeep was nearly as good as a Ferrari. I of course said, "Sure, I can drive the stuff over to the other 40 with the Jeep. I'll come back to the marsh and pick up Dave before going back to the house."

"You're sure you know how to drive it?" Bob reiterated.

"Sure, I know how to drive it." After all, that was what any self-respecting male would say, regardless of whether he was stretching the truth or outright lying. It was what men do. Even at my tender age I knew that obnoxious male trait backward and forward. We can do ANYTHING, and will state that it is so! It goes back to the first caveman jumping on a sabre-toothed tiger when his buddy dared him to ride that big pussy cat. Although that one probably didn't turn out too well.

They undid the tractor, hooked up the Jeep to the side rake with the hay lifter and an empty wagon behind it and took off for the marsh. For my part, I had never so much as sat in the seat of a Jeep before and now I was going to drive one. I was so excited I forgot about anything else except that I was going to get to drive a real car-like vehicle! The first couple of times I tried to put it in gear a god-awful grinding reminded me that this clutch was a bit more sensitive than the Allis Chalmers tractor transmission. When I final got the hang of it and slowly in first gear got everything moving I put in the clutch and shifted to second. More grinding. On the third try I got it in but by now the speed had dropped so much second gear merely stalled out trying to pull the three pieces of equipment behind me. This learning curve was a little steeper than I had anticipated but I doggedly kept trying, shortening the life of the Jeep tranny and clutch considerably I am sure. Thank heavens, Bob and Dave were a quarter of a mile away and could not hear my embarrassing grinding.

    The good news is that I final got it and in second gear I was traveling at a mind-boggling nine or ten miles an hour over the now freshly gleaned hay field headed for the other big hayfield. The smile on my face could not be measured as I thought to myself, "What's the big deal with driving? It's easy!" As I turned to my right to cross over the humplike bridge that spanned the 15 foot wide McCann stream I did slow down because I was pulling big pieces of equipment. I knew I had to speed up a bit to get over the bridge hump with the Jeep, but when on the other side I stepped on the brakes, very little happened. Eighty feet of metal machinery behind me had a certain momentum I had not figured into the equation. When my train did stop, I looked back and panic flooded my entire being. I had not taken the turn wide enough and now the rake and lifter were on the downside of the bridge albeit close to the edge . . .

but the wagon was just approaching the top of the bridge hump and the front right wheel was already OFF the edge! If I went five feet further, the entire wagon would slide off into the stream and probably tip the hay lifter with it as well.

Thinking I could fix this by backing up a little bit, I was mistaken on two counts. First, putting the Jeep in reverse and letting the clutch out easy did nothing but make wheels spin on the Jeep. Nothing moved an inch. Even had I been able to get something to move backwards, I had no clue as to which direction any of the towed pieces of equipment would go. That's when I shut off the engine and decided a closer look was called for in this situation. Walking back and alternately pushing and pulling on various sections provided no answers and even less movement.

Then I had a brilliant idea. If I could get the whole train moving forward fast enough, I could simply pull the wagon over the bridge even if part of it was sliding into the water. The obvious key was to have enough speed to pull everything out and over the bank of the stream. It was only a couple of feet high anyway and a mass of bushes would cushion the wheel bounce! Feeling like the light at the end of the tunnel had just appeared, I climbed back into the driver's seat of the Jeep. Rev the engine high, I reminded myself, so I could get enough speed in the next fifteen or twenty feet and everything would be O.K! To this day, I cannot recall both Dave and Bob running toward the mess from fifty yards behind me, screaming at the top of their lungs and frantically waving their arms.

I neither saw nor heard anything but the semi-mufflered roar of a vintage 1951 Willys Jeep revving over its redline as I let out the clutch. Amazingly, the whole train moved forward, gaining a bit of speed for several seconds . . . and then everything devolved into super slow motion. The Jeep stopped moving forward and began to go backward slowly even as the wheels wildly spun forward, spitting gravel in every direction. When I turned around to see the results of my brilliant idea, (there was no rear view mirror) the rear of the empty hay wagon was hidden because it was already down in the stream bed and the 18 foot tall hay lifter in front of the wagon was lazily drifting over on its side, half in the very same stream bed where the wagon resided.

In Cousin Bob's defence, the only thing he said to me was, "Boy, I don't think your Pa or my Pa will be happy about this." Before we heard the tractor roaring back in road gear, we saw Uncle Roy's Pontiac screaming toward us along the dirt road, kicking up a monstrous cloud of dust. No one said a word as all the men slowly walked around the entire disaster. I stood off to the side as far from the Jeep as I could get. When we had all gathered together, Uncle Roy asked, "What happened?"

Dave started to blurt, "I was . . . "

But Bob rode over him and said, "I'm sorry but it was my fault. I told Roger to take the equipment over to this field so we could get an early start tomorrow. It was all my fault. Sorry, Pa."

There was a pregnant pause for what I thought was minutes but am sure it was no more than five or ten seconds. What were they going to do? Scream bloody murder at a 12-year-old? Uncle Roy was a harsh man. I expected it and certainly deserved that much at the least. Everyone was staring at the ground as the silence lengthened, when I glanced up at Pa. He was staring at me. I was pretty sure there was steam coming out of his ears. His progeny had just screwed up royally. But there was something else in his eyes. Almost a questioning look. A look of expectation. Then it hit me. I had not said one word the entire time they were all here. And I was the driver who did this!

"Wait," I spoke up nearly in tears, with my voice breaking, "It's my fault. Not Bob's. He asked me if I knew how to drive the Jeep. I said sure. I can drive it. I lied. I said I did. I never drove anything but the Allis tractor. I really wanted to drive a Jeep. I thought I could. Really! I did! I am so sorry. Sorry! Sorry! "

At which point, Uncle Roy came over to me and put his hand on my shoulder and said, "We'll get her all sorted out in the morning. Let's go have supper." It was as close to emotion as I ever experienced then or after from my Uncle Roy. Pa put his arms around me as he and I walked the long mile all the way back to the farmhouse alone. The only admonition I heard from Pa was, "You know your cousin Bob trusted you to be truthful, don't you?"

"Yes, I know," I replied, holding back the tears.

"You let him down. When people trust you, the very worst thing you can do, as a man, is to let them down. Don't do it again."

Then, as the setting sun burnt the Wisconsin sky into a striking orange, Pa stopped in the middle of that dusty dirt farm road, turned to me, leaned over and hugged me.

Lesson Four

Funny Depends on What Side of the Fence You're On

The wandering three-holer

Running With the Big Dogs

During those preteen years when I spent many glorious weeks and months up on my Uncle Roy's small dairy farm, I remember with clarity Pa reminding me to keep my own council and to keep in mind that my three cousins, Bob, Dave and Rolly were considerably older than I was and I should not attempt to run with the big dogs. I thought this saying humorous, but could not grasp why I should have to be warned about the dogs. I had been around dogs on the farm many times and we all got along just great. And all of the farm dogs were big.

The first few years that we traveled the 120 miles to the "Farm," as it was known to me, was more like camping than anything else. Although the farmhouse had running water, cooking and heating were provided by wood burning stoves and heaters. Most summer days my bothersome little brother and I spent outdoors exploring the "vast" 120 acres of an exotic ecosystem far different than our city home could provide. During the summers, because my aunt and my mom were just two of nine sisters, we often had other cousins with us for visits as well. Sometimes our numbers would swell to a small herd. My father and my uncles and our families would often show up to help with the plowing, milking and a myriad of other farm tasks that needed extra hands.

We kids played never-ending games of War with four decks of cards on the huge screened-in porch after dinner and we actually looked forward to bedtime because we got to sleep in the hay barns without any adult supervision. It was nirvana for us kids with one exception: the outhouse.

    The three-holer (large, medium, small) was a rickety ramshackle shed leaning as if to fall over any moment, and surrounded by a rotted wooden fence to prevent one from accidentally slipping into the huge pit that showed around the edges of the "throne room." The walls of wood slats were so unevenly spaced that moonlight easily illuminated the interior at night in spite of a closed door. Not that any of us ever wanted to be in that place after the sun went down and the spiders took over! The interior was infested with all manner of insects, but none so terrifying to us kids as the spiders. Certainly more unpleasant for my girl cousins than for us boys who came equipped with outdoor plumbing, it was a place none of us lingered any more than absolutely necessary in spite of a wide selection of outdated Sears catalogs displaying women in underwear. Winters were a different matter. Freezing cold and snow were just one more adventure for an eleven-year-old but certain death to the buzzing and web-spinning inhabitants of the three-holer. That fact made it tolerable regardless of the icy drafts that blew through the interior, unimpeded by the haphazardly spaced boards.

    My Uncle Roy was a man of mystery to me. Married to my mother's sister, Aunt Sophie, he was part Cherokee Indian and part granite stone. Stoic, and a man of few spoken words, he nevertheless instilled a sense of fear in us younger cousins, but less so in his own three boys, I learned to my chagrin. We had no reason to account for this feeling because he rarely spoke to us and never once that I can ever remember in anger. He was mystifying because he was unlike our other uncles who we often saw overtly gregarious after a few beers at our frequent family get-togethers. I never saw him with a bottle of beer. A thin wiry man of amazing energy, he was always the first to return to the chores after eating, the last to quit upon hearing the evening dinner bell. He was also a man of habit. Rising at six on the dot every day of the year, he kept to a schedule for every minute of his day, including an evening trek the thirty yards to the Throne Room every night at 10:30, rain, sleet or snow. It was this habit that provided me the insight to my father's admonition about running with the big dogs.

I idolized my older cousins and lived for any semblance of recognition from them other than "get this" or "go there." One early December day after deer season, I came upon them sneaking smokes in the milk house pump room. I heard laughter but as I entered, they stopped and looked at me. They knew I would never snitch on them for smoking but there was something else in the air as they glanced at each other. I was shocked but enormously elated when they asked if I wanted to help them with a joke they were going to play on their Dad. I immediately agreed without ever asking what kind of help they needed. Could I sneak out of bed and meet back at the milk house at 10:00 p.m. sharp? Could I? Wow! Of course I could and it would be easy! The farmhouse was huge, with three doors to the outside and my room that trip was at the rear end making it easy for me to slip out without the adults who would be talking and smoking in the kitchen next to the big wood burning stove seeing or hearing me.

  At the appointed time I dressed in warm clothes and my winter jacket I had previously stashed in my room and quietly made my way out the rear entrance. It had been bitter cold for the previous week but tonight a moonless night seemed warm by comparison and a few snowflakes fluttered down to paint the paths white under the yard light. As I crept toward the milk house the yard light snapped out on timer and I was momentarily blinded by the darkness. Three glowing cigarette tips acted as my beacon to the milk house and the cousins quickly outlined the plan. We were going to move the outhouse/throne room back about two feet so that when Uncle Roy made his nightly journey in the dark he'd step into the gap and get his boots "brown." We'd all jump out and yell "surprise" and then run like hell. Any misgivings I had were overshadowed by the older cousin's laughter at what a surprise awaited their Dad.

  The outhouse was so flimsy it required very little effort (almost none by me) to move it a couple of feet and we all retired to our hiding places that Bob had pre-assigned. I did notice mine was next to the woodshed directly opposite the outhouse only 20 feet away. With the yard light out the only illumination was a faint reflection off the snow from the kitchen windows many feet away. As 10:30 approached my uncle came out and shuffled his way to the Throne Room, his snow boots slipping and sliding in the thin carpet of fresh snow. I felt as if he would hear my heart thumping so loudly as he passed within ten feet of me but without seeing me, he turned and went to open the door of the outhouse. I heard a loud "THWOMP" and then a screaming string of words I had never heard before. I waited to the count of three as Bob and Dave and Rolly said we were to do and then I jumped out and yelled "SURPRISE!" The biggest surprise, however, was that I was the only one jumping out and yelling "surprise."

Uncle Roy had fallen nearly up to his waist into the gap but was already out by the time I was done yelling "surprise." More words loudly emanated from him that I did not know. I forgot to run. I do know his boots were not "brown" because his yelling had brought the house awake and the overhead yard light brightly outlined a terrified 11-year-old too afraid to run, too naïve to understand the concept of betrayal, and staring at boots that were decidedly not "brown."

It was obvious to the adults I could not have moved the outhouse by myself and my cousins stayed really low key for the next few days. My personal penance for being "in on it," was to collect the eggs every morning until we returned to the city. It was a job I hated most of all because those darn hens would peck at me unmercifully, drawing tiny droplets of blood 20 or 30 times every morning. The only comment directed to me that I remember from my father was, "Guess the big dogs had the last laugh, huh?" I think he was chuckling. I got the point. That growing-up lesson was one of the very few that soaked in immediately and stayed with me for a lifetime. Let the Big Dogs run but remember you are just a little dog in the greater scheme of things.

Lesson Five
I AM my brother's keeper

The famous flying toboggan in earlier times

Deadman's Hill

M<small>OST</small> YEARS, January arrives with a shiver in central Wisconsin. A biting cold carried down from the Canadian Arctic into the upper Midwest by the relentless wind known as the Alberta Clipper not only freezes the fertile fields of our little dairy farm in Waushara County, it jellifies the flow of daily life as well. There remains nearly as much work to do as during warmer months but there is no time constraint or any rush to repair the aging hay baler before next summer's first cutting. And so for those of us youngsters on the cusp of a productive farm working age, winter repairs are a man's work and not required attendance for us boys. The frozen months present an opportunity for much midday recreation unfettered by farm chores. There is still the twice a day routine of feeding and milking the cows, of course, but field work is nearly nonexistent except for the spreading of manure on the frozen turf of next year's cornfields.

Such was the winter when my much younger brother, Tom, was given a flashy new winter coat for a Christmas present. Like all older brothers, I was in a state of constant irritation over his seemingly "easier" path in life than my own at his age. I would inflict as much pain on him as I could reasonably get away with before the wrath of Pa fell on me or the fear of same brought sense to my evil machinations. Pa's only admonition to me was always the same. "He's your only brother. Don't cross over the line." What line? And how would I know if I ever crossed it? Regardless, as the fear of Pa's wrath receded, and it always did, my ingenuity for damaging my pest of a brother increased in an inverse proportion.

    One of the most irritating of my brother's traits was his uncanny ability to divine my intentions to go tobogganing. No matter how secretive I was about making preparations, he would somehow guess my intentions and immediately demand to go along. I would say no and he would appeal to a higher court, our mom. Ma would always say no, reiterating that he was too small to be off in the woods with the big boys. And I would do that silent "nyah, nyah, nyah" thing to him behind Ma's back. Happily, that would infuriate him and totally make my day. However, on this particular day, the words out of Ma's mouth were more chilling than the zero degrees showing on the thermometer.

    "Tommy, I think you're big enough now. Roger, you take your brother along today and watch out for him because he's still smaller than the rest of you boys. And stay away from Deadman's Hill."

    In my mind I screamed, "EXACTLY why he should NOT go along with us! He's just TOO SMALL!" But the only thing that came out of my mouth was a wimpy, whiny, "But Mom!" One did not scream or raise one's voice to our mom, particularly if within earshot of Pa, that is, if one wished to avoid the aforementioned wrath. My brother, sensing his

Lesson Five

newfound power base, swiftly demanded to wear his brand new Christmas coat because it was warmer than his old one. Once again that little weasel wins the prize and Ma agrees to his wishes because it is "pretty chilly out" today. I want to kill him for ruining my adventure with the guys. Especially since we were planning to confront Deadman's Hill today. Pa and Ma, and my uncle whose land it was situated on, always issued the same old "don't go there" warning every single time we took out the toboggan. We always said, "Of course we won't go there." And then, of course, we always went there.

    So, off we trudged across a corn-stubble strewn field to Danny's house, our breaths trailing locomotive-like clouds of steam in the still air. The sharp crackling of our boots on the frozen snow was punctuated only by the swish-swish of Weasel's snow-pants rubbing together as he waddled alongside the toboggan. Alongside, because no way am I going to let the Weasel ride while I pulled. If he wants to play with the big boys he can walk like the rest of us. A small penance he well deserves for forcing his way into our private club! Twenty minutes later Danny, my cousin Jack, I and the Weasel are marching resolutely into the back forty big woods where the best toboggan hill in all of central Wisconsin silently awaited its next victims.

    Deadman's Hill was infamous in our area for several reasons, not the least of which was the rock ledge about a third of the way down the long, steep hill. It had a sheer drop of about twenty feet, but as snow accumulated in the lee of the cliff over the course of a winter's storms, it looked to be much less of a drop. However, standing at the bottom and looking up, it was nonetheless heart-stopping for us preteens. Many stories abound about flying off the ledge in total control only to terrifyingly disintegrate into chaos as a toboggan loaded with screaming kids crashes upside down into the snowy hillside.

    The steep lower downhill run, which could be blazingly fast, allowing a run all the way to the adjacent cornfield a couple of hundred yards further away, was rarely experienced by any of the story-tellers because few ever landed rightside up after launching off of the cliff ledge. Oh, I suppose one could have steered around the ledge, but of course that option never really occurred to any of us. We had often done the run starting below the cliff but at this point in our lives, that was considered only for babies. Deadman's Hill was only about the cliff jump. And digging each other out of a frozen snow bank after another failed attempt was important fodder for our youthful tales of bravery. It was the ledge than made it Deadman's Hill. It was the ledge that was the bestower of "guts." It was the ledge where legends were born anew.

    On this day, when we arrived at the base of the looming hill, the Weasel looked up to the black smudge that was the underside of the rock ledge and exclaimed, "Hey, wait a minute. This is Deadman's Hill, isn't it? Remember? Pa said we couldn't go here."

    "Nah," I replied, winking at Danny. "This isn't Deadman's Hill. That's on the other side. This hill is O.K. for you."

"Wow," he quivered, "Looks really big. And all those bushes and trees. How do we steer around them if we're going so fast?"

"Hey Weasel, you wanted to come along. Maybe that new jacket should be yellow instead of gray," Jack snorted.

We three laughed and started up the hill with a chastised Weasel bringing up the rear reluctantly, but at least without his constant chatter. It hadn't snowed for a few days and the surface crust was still frozen hard because the sun wouldn't reach this side of the hill until much later in the day, if at all. An icy crust would propel the toboggan at warp speed. Absolutely perfect toboggan conditions. Today's runs would certainly be the stuff of legend and we'd all have the rides of our lives! Today was definitely going to be the day!

The snap and crunch of six leather booted high tops breaking through the frozen crust measured our assent to the top of the hill. The Weasel wore his dull black snow boots with the metal buckle fasteners from last year, once again a visual reminder that he was not one of us. After all, leather hightops with laces all the way up nearly to your knees was the footwear of choice for any self-respecting adventurer. It WAS the only boot Frank Buck would ever wear during his adventures in his book, "Bring 'Em Back Alive!."

Which, of course, was the primary reason the TV show of the same name never took off. Every kid in the world knew those boots would keep him safe from poisonous spider bites, venomous snakes and even would save his life if and when a croc snapped at his leg. Bruce Boxleitner played Frank Buck in the TV version and never wore those high tops. That's how we all KNEW it was a huge fake. If it were real, he wouldn't have dared to stomp around in jungles without the protection of those leather hightops. End of discussion.

A ways up the hill we stopped briefly to catch our breath and inspect the rock face we would soon be flying over at unbelievable speeds. The three of us had all gone off this launch ramp a bunch of times. Of course, we had never successfully landed and continued on down the hill, but we firmly believed the stories of those who claimed they had. We believed it was not only possible, but mandatory if one wanted to be counted among the select few. Those few whose bravery was beyond question. Those few whose acquired scars would serve as a badge of courage to any and all who might otherwise doubt your toughness. And so with manhood at stake, particularly in front of your buddies, over the cliff it was.

The dirty little secret we all kept to ourselves was that we were all terrified of this hill, this jump and the inevitable death roll of the toboggan as it re-entered the atmosphere and actually struck the snowy hillside some 30 feet down range . . . usually upside down. The only clue to this universal reticence was the marked slowing of footsteps the last 75 yards up the hill after the cliff face. Some of us more imaginative climbers would needlessly breathe slightly harder so as to give reason to our slowing steps.

Lesson Five

    I remember clearly our first encounter with "Deadman." It was a warm sunny late March afternoon and the snow was wet, soft, and deep. We pushed off the top, Danny in front, my cousin Jack in the center and myself bringing up the rear as the toboggan slowly accelerated down the sticky slope toward the launch point. With all of us screaming at the top of our lungs, the edge of the ledge approaching, our fears mounting, we were incapable of realizing just how slow we were going.

    In a burst of speed just before the edge, we flew off the ledge at a blazing one mile an hour. And then . . . completely stopped! Now, with the front of the toboggan and Danny dangling over the edge in midair, Jack and I, with only a second or two of hesitation, jerked our bodies forward to get us moving again just as we always did on sticky snow. Big mistake. The toboggan inched forward, immediately nosed down and did a complete flip as it simply dropped off the ledge. Being consummate tobogganers, we all grimly held on for the entire two seconds of air launch, subsequent midair flip, and then landed head first in the snow bank at the bottom of the cliff, toboggan above us, still attached to our butts and held firmly in place by our locked arms and legs. That was our first attempt at glory. Lesson learned. Stay off the launch ramp when the snow was sticky.

    We'd had other attempts in better snow conditions, but all had ended in a similarly disastrous manner. And for good reason. As one approached the very edge, the land sloped a bit to the left and so as you left the launch point, the toboggan was forced into beginning a spiral just as a football leaving the passer's hand. Our sophisticated teamwork had yet to advance to the stage where our combined body shift and leaning would override and compensate for this tendency to "death-roll." In fact, the curved bow of the toboggan sported a nasty crack in one of the staves where it had encountered a small tree upon re-entry. We, of course thought it humorous, unlike my uncle who demanded to know how we cracked the stave in his prized 12-foot meticulously varnished toboggan. "Must have struck a rock" we all chortled.

But today we were confident. Sure, the Weasel was a complication but he didn't weigh much and sticking him between Jack and me at the back of the toboggan would negate his lack of experience. We had it figured. Fast snow, experienced riders, and glory awaiting us a mere 75 yards down the slope. With the crusty conditions today, we would have no problem overcoming the slow start normal for the top of Deadman. The slope was nearly flat at the top, necessitating that the three of us run alongside and push just as bobsledders do to get a fast start. Then each one hops aboard, Danny in the front slot first, so he could begin steering, then Jack intertwining his legs around Danny in front of him and finally me climbing aboard last and also locking my legs into Jack's position. A single unified and determined team braving the unknown.

We'd decided that the Weasel would sit between Jack and me at the back so we needed only to figure out how I could lock him into our team as we picked up speed toward the ledge. He already knew about holding on to the bolt rope along each edge for dear life so that part of the equation had been solved. We prepared at the top by setting him where we thought he should be and then we all climbed aboard to show him how we fit together as a unit while we roared down the hill. For once the Weasel wasn't saying anything at all. In fact, he looked a little green, just as he often did before he upchucked the brussels sprouts he hated so much at the dinner table. But we were having none of it. He wanted to barge into our club and so be it. He was in for the whole show now. We had punched his ticket to ride. And it was definitely going to be the E-Ticket ride!

While the Weasel remained seated on the toboggan we three got off, patted each other on the back for courage, took our standing start positions and gave a big yell as we pushed off downhill. The toboggan took off with little resistance on the crusted snow and Danny jumped aboard within just a few steps. Obviously we would not need to push much so Jack climbed aboard immediately thereafter. I would have done the same but the toboggan was now moving much faster than I had anticipated and I stumbled attempting to get on. In a last ditch effort I managed to dive chest first onto the back of the toboggan behind the Weasel. Danny and Jack were whooping at the top of their lungs about how fast we were going, but I was desperately trying to climb back into a sitting position before we got to the ledge takeoff. When I finally got into position, I looked up and was stunned to see how fast we were moving. However, I had no time to think about this as immediately I heard Danny screaming, "Heeere weeee goooo!" And the toboggan literally leapt off the ledge into the wild, cold blue yonder.

Danny yelled out the all important "LLEEAAN NOOOW!," and we all leaned our bodies to the right. And miracle of miracles . . . our rocket ship straightened out in midair and we were FLYING LEVEL! And right-side up. This had never happened before. All of us were screaming at the top of our lungs when my lucky hat flew off my head. I didn't care. This was worth a whole winter of disastrous rides! We would make history today!

The five or six seconds we were in the air seemed an eternity to me and as we approached the landing spot we all braced ourselves for the impact. Deadman was fairly steep at the impact point so it was more of a glancing blow than a direct impact but in our exuberance at being above the toboggan for once and not beneath it, we failed to notice the slight tipping of our craft as we struck the hard crusted surface snow. The right edge chipped through the crust first, throwing up a huge spray of granular crystals. This was immediately followed by a blossoming cloud of powdery under-snow that totally obscured our vision for a few more seconds. When a deafening scream or two confirmed we were all still aboard, the toboggan blasted through the snow cloud and shot down the lower hillside at phenomenal speed.

Lesson Five

With the clearing of the snow cloud from our faces, Danny realized first, followed instantly by Jack and myself that we were not going down the wide open hillside as we expected, but instead headed directly for the forest edge. In a desperate attempt to correct our course, Danny called for a hard lean to our left in a vain attempt to get us back on course. For those not familiar with the technical aspects of our rocket ship, a toboggan has relatively little steering control. You can adjust your course a few degrees one way or the other, but they are intended for open hillsides, not a dense forest dotted with tree trunks thick and thin.

As we shot across the icy snow far faster than we had ever gone before, the increasing hiss of the ash slats on frozen snow became ominous. After another thirty yards, it became frighteningly clear we would not be able to steer clear of the woods. We did not panic. Actually, we were prepared for this eventuality, having practiced it, albeit at much slower speeds. It was a simple command from Danny at the front who would yell out "Dump, one, two, three," at which point we would all simultaneously roll off the toboggan to opposite sides. As we rapidly approached the brambles and wild raspberry patch directly ahead of us, Danny yelled out the order to dump. On the three count, we all neatly rolled off the toboggan. Except, that is, for the Weasel. We'd forgotten that he didn't know about the dump code. He was riding to his demise with both hands in a death grip on the bolt rope!

"JUUMMPP!" we all yelled in unison. But the Weasel was glued to that toboggan. We knew he could hear us but he would not let go of that careening missile. He and the toboggan entered the wild raspberry patch at warp speed and they both disappeared into the underbrush. Now we could hear the Weasel screaming and it was not from excitement. It was the excruciating squeal of pain. As we three ran willy-nilly down the hill toward the patch, miraculously the toboggan shot out of the brambles on the far side. And more miraculously, it had veered while in the raspberry brambles and was now headed directly down the center of our open hillside!

Furthermore, the Weasel was still attached. True, he was now lying flat on his back, screaming, but he was still on the toboggan! As we ran toward him we suddenly realized we would never be able to catch up with him. Although slowed considerably by the bramble patch, now that it was once again on frozen unobstructed snow facing down a steep hill, the toboggan was rapidly accelerating. This was not good news. It was totally out of control and without anyone at least trying to steer it. The Weasel remained flat on his back emitting one long continuous scream.

We ran as crazy fast as we could and yelled at him to jump off but his own screams drowned out our warnings. We watched helplessly as the toboggan and its charge roared down Lower Deadman toward the waiting cornfield . . . and the barbed wire fence that bordered it. My heart pounding, I passed Jack and Danny and ran faster than I ever knew I could, knowing full well that the Weasel was going to get to that three-strand barbed wire fence long before I could get there. By the time the toboggan reached the fence, it had slowed considerably. As the front slid effortlessly under the barbed wire it came to a halt. My brother was not screaming anymore.

When we raced up to the toboggan, the lower strand of barbed wire was stretched across my little brother's chest about three inches from his head. His entire face was covered in blood as was his new winter coat. He was softly crying but his hands had released the toboggan's bolt rope and were gingerly grasping a strand of barbed wire immediately above him. There was more human blood than any of us three had ever seen before. We tenderly slid him out from under the fence and then while he laid very still on the toboggan, we three galloped the three-quarters of a mile to the farmhouse pulling the wounded boy nearly as fast as he had ridden down Deadman's Hill.

As is sometimes the case with kids who do dumb things, we were lucky. All of Tommy's wounds were shallow scratches from brambles and raspberry canes. None were deep or scar-producing. The new winter coat, however, was another story. It took the brunt of the brambles and it was shredded beyond recognition. The blood stains made it a gruesome sight to boot, and it was quickly relegated to the trash heap. An hour later, once the furor of what we had done to Tom had eased a bit, Pa sat me down and simply said, "You were supposed to protect your brother. You crossed the line. You know that don't you?"

My tears, suffused as they were with fear for my brother as well as for myself, easily told the truth of it. I had crossed the line. And now I knew exactly where the line lay.

My banishment from the toboggan for the rest of that winter as punishment for not being my brother's keeper was extremely painful. And yet, even more painful was the realization that the only one of us who would ever be able to claim he had ridden Deadman's Hill from the very top, over the ledge, and all the way to the cornfield on the bottom, was my own little baby brother. Throughout our lives, the Weasel has never let me forget that fact. And I never went back for my lucky hat.

Lesson Six
Danger Not Only Lurks, It Grabs

The silo and Pa feeding corn into the chopper

Hot Hand, Cool Head

When you are a man of 11 or 12 or 13, few things are as irritating as an adult telling you to be careful. During those years when I spent a great deal of time on the small dairy farm owned by my aunt and uncle in central Wisconsin, I had my aunt, my uncle, my three cousins, my mother, and of course Pa, all reminding me of the multitude of dangers lurking just beyond my recognition. Well, du-uh. Of course, I would be careful. I didn't like pain any more than anyone else and not being careful meant pain. It even sometimes meant pain when you WERE being careful. So why did they have to keep reminding me? After all, we had plenty of Band-Aids and at least a dozen of those little bottles of that red stuff that caused more actual pain than the cut or scratch it was fixing.

The year I learned what being careful truly meant was the year I, for the very first time in my life, saw pain, blood, bravery, panic, and heroism all in a few short minutes, up close and personal. It would not be my last exposure to those events, but some seminal days and some seminal events stay with us for all the years of our lives and we can moan and groan about them, dismiss them or deny them, but they WILL shape who we are as individuals whether we want them to or not.

September/October is corn harvesting season in central Wisconsin. On the small dairy farm I knew, we harvested not only whole ears that had been left on the stalk in the field to dry until after the first frost, but mostly whole corn stalks for silage. Silage was the entire stalk, the leaves, AND the ears chopped up into tiny pieces while still green and moist and blown up and into silos. Those tall silos that are so ubiquitous to midwestern America's fertile farmland scenes kept the chopped corn moist and warm all winter, providing our small herd of dairy cows with their daily greens.

The process was just a tad Rube Goldberg-like because farm equipment in those days was not self-propelled and did not have any engine or motors on board. Rather, all motive power for its moving parts was derived from a tractor's PTO (power take-off) wheel and the drive wheel on the equipment being run. The connection between the two was an eight-inch wide circular belt that spanned the twenty-five or thirty feet between the two pieces of machinery. It was incredibly noisy (think of those tree branch choppers in your city but five times as loud), and dangerous, if you got too close to the huge belt that was spinning at 25 or 30 miles per hour as it spun around the steel PTO wheels.

When a wagon load of freshly-cut corn stalks arrived at the chopper/blower next to the silo being filled, I would rush inside the silo with my pitchfork and spread the silage as it piled up in the center of the silo. I know some folks will call it foolish because it was not truly a necessary job but as kids we loved being in the corn "rainfall." Today, of course, OSHA

Lesson Six

would cringe at the thought of a youngster in a filling silo, worried that the oxygen level would decrease and render anyone in the silo unconscious. With all entrances to the silo from inside and the roof, it was not a danger we ever gave thought to and besides, one wagon load of corn would take only 10 to 15 minutes to chop and then we would have another hour wait outside for the wagon to return with another load to chop.

    On the day that is forever indelibly marked in my memory I had just started to spread the silage when the "corn rain" stopped unexpectedly. The roar from the equipment running outside prevented me from hearing much but after a few moments and no corn silage showering down on me, I climbed out of the silo to see what was happening. I exited the silo through the ground opening into the cow barn and then walked the 20 or 30 yards around to the outside, when the noise of the tractor and the chopper went silent. I heard Pa and my uncle talking. As I got a little closer, Pa saw me and yelled at me to run to the machine shed and get a crowbar. And run fast! Both Pa and Uncle Roy were standing up on the chopper leaning over the feed trough where the two steel grinding wheels first crushed the corn stalks before the chopper cut them into small pieces. I spun on my heels and made a beeline for the machine shed a hundred feet away, grabbed the biggest crowbar on the tool wall and ran back. Pa reached over, grabbed the crowbar, and again yelled at me to run to the house, get my aunt and the car. Bring two or three clean towels as well. I stood there transfixed as panic began to freeze my thoughts.

At least seven or eight minutes had passed since I noticed the corn had stopped falling on my head and at least another three or four minutes passed while I came out and ran to the tool shed to bring the crowbar. Pa noticed me out of the corner of his eye standing and not moving. He slammed the crowbar on the side of the chopper, causing a loud clang and screamed at me to get moving. That sudden clang and his voice jolted me out of my panic-induced frozen state and I flew back to the farmhouse. During the brief glimpse of Uncle Roy wincing and panting looking up to the sky, I heard Pa say in a calm, soothing voice, "Hang on, hang on, I almost got them open." I ran like crazy, terrified because I knew something was drastically wrong. I just didn't know exactly what. I was running back to the chopper carrying an arm full of towels with my aunt following as quickly as she could, her apron flying off behind her, to drive the car to the chopper. That's when I figured it out.

I climbed up quickly to the chopper next to Pa and my uncle. Sure enough, I could not see my uncle's hand. It had disappeared into and between the steel rollers at the feeder trough. My uncle's eyes were rolling up into his head and he was moaning while Pa kept talking, "Almost got it . . . just a little more . . . hang on, Roy."

I heard a sharp metallic crack and my uncle suddenly flew backward, landing on the still loaded corn stalks not yet chopped, holding his wrist. All I could see of his hand was a bloody red mess. Pa jumped down after him immediately and wrapped the towels around his hand, all the time talking to Roy. A moment or two later Pa half carried my uncle, placing him in the passenger seat, running around to the driver's side while my aunt got in the back seat. Uncle Roy was murmuring but Pa kept talking to him, making Roy answer him. As they roared out of the driveway, Pa yelled back at me to disconnect the belt between the tractor and the corn chopper.

Morbid curiosity made me climb back up on the chopper to look carefully at the offending rollers. They were perhaps two inches apart on one side and at a crazy angle. At nearly two feet wide and nine inches in diameter with a normal even gap of only three-eighths inch between them, I shivered to think a hand had passed through that tiny gap. It was then I noticed the crowbar jammed in the end of the rollers. Pa had, with superhuman strength, pried apart the rollers, snapping the solid steel nine inch gear wheel to make the gap and pull out the hand.

In times of extreme stress, people react in radically different ways. Some freeze, some scream, some close their eyes and some act. Everyone has heard of the superman-like exploits of an average person lifting a car to free a trapped victim. Pa broke a solid steel gear wheel that probably weighed in at seven or eight pounds using his bare hands and a rusty crowbar. In retrospect, a couple of things were clearly brought home to me that afternoon.

First, when the hand was caught by the crushing rollers, the glove he was wearing gave a few moments for my uncle to yell above the din to my father, who immediately saw the disaster unfolding. He jumped down from the corn wagon to the bed of the chopper and manually pulled the lever to take it out of gear. Although this stopped the steel wheels from dragging more of my Uncle into those unrelenting jaws, in those few moments, the machine had eaten the glove and the hand up to the wrist. The hand was unmercifully mashed to unrecognizability and would very soon have to be amputated.

Secondly, had my Uncle not recognized his predicament instantly and yelled to my father, had Pa not instantly reacted and jumped the six feet down to the chopper bed and thrown the gear lever, had my uncle not remained conscious while unbelievable pain surged through him, the outcome, as gruesome as it was, could easily have been fatal. Two men, both horrendously stressed, without thinking, without weighing options, without regard to personal safety, acted instantaneously together to save a life.

Accidents happen on farms every day. Some less dramatic, some more so and some fatal. Danger lurks whenever and wherever large machinery is running. Until that fateful day, I never thought about the danger of the machinery, only the efficiency it brought to the small dairy farm in central Wisconsin. I found it so mechanically fascinating. Yes, danger did lurk there but worse for my uncle, it grabbed as well.

Lesson Seven
Women Rarely Say What They Mean

My brother Tom with me sporting remnants of the portage trail trip

Walking on Eggs

My folks fervently believed in family vacations. As did my brother and I, until our teens of course. Our vacations always started some cold and rainy spring morning when my father would drag up from the basement, the fifteen-gallon pickling crock he used as our vacation bank account. All year long, whenever he passed the crock he would reach deep into his pockets, pull out all the loose change, and toss it into the crock. Even my brother and I would reluctantly toss in a nickel or dime from our weekly 25 cent allowance, knowing that the more money in the crock the more fun we'd have on summer vacation. Pa never suggested or even mentioned that we should contribute, but I felt he noticed and smiled when we did.

There was magic in the anticipation as we spent hours counting and stacking the pennies, nickels, dimes, quarters and half dollars from the huge pile in the middle of our kitchen table. It was often complicated by the fact that my much younger brother could neither count nor stack coins without spreading a considerable number of them on the floor. I realized years later that of course the 90 or 100 dollars we counted out was not nearly enough for our various vacations, but Ma and Pa mostly watched and chuckled as me and my brother reveled in finding the occasional half dollar or even a rare silver dollar!

We were a working-class family and money was often dear so the fact that my mother had eight sisters scattered all over the country meant we had a place to stay in exotic (to us) locations whenever we did a car trip vacation. One of my favorite places to visit was my Aunt Jo and Uncle Matt's home in Ely, Minnesota. They were both avid outdoor people, hunting, fishing and camping along the border with Canada and into what is currently known as the Boundry Waters Canoe area. At that time, we knew it under the exotic name, Quetico. I drank in their stories of wilderness camping and canoeing with an insatiable thirst.

Begging to experience it myself, I convinced Ma and Pa to ask Aunt Jo and Uncle Matt if, as our big yearly vacation, they would guide us into that Canadian wilderness they knew so well. When Aunt Jo wrote back saying they would love to take us out for a week or so, I was ecstatic. Thus my entire spring that year was infused with thoughts of paddling canoes, of campfires, catching fish and swimming in crystal clear waters under sunny skies and starry nights.

When the interminable June and July months finally slipped behind me, Ma and Pa loaded up the big Buick and we headed far beyond northern Wisconsin and into God's Country. Destination: that exotic and exciting wilderness known as Canada. Upon arriving in Ely, we spent a couple of days visiting with all my mom's relatives prior to our weeklong canoe trip. Those days dragged slowly but my Uncle

Lesson Seven

Matt, sensing a certain impatience on my part, took action. He was a gruff sort of man who worked most of his life in the iron ore mines on the Messabi Range and yet could be incredibly patient teaching youngsters the beauties of the wilderness and the outdoors. I recall with fondness how he took several hours one of those days to explain, demonstrate and teach me how to sight in a rifle without ever firing a bullet! I dined out on that story, amazing my buddies at the school lunch table for years afterward.

When our two families finally sat down to plan real logistics, it was shocking to me how much I did not know beyond having read every book in our city library about canoeing. How much food we would have to carry in, how many canoes we needed for the seven of us, because my cousin from Milwaukee was with us. It was a lot! Far more than I would or could have imagined. Yet, it was all needed for a comfortable vacation. Who knew we'd have to bring four dozen eggs, pounds and pounds of bacon, flour, butter, spices, hot dogs, several bags of marshmallows and all the pots and pans and silverware for seven! It appeared to me as though we would be carrying the entire kitchen pantry on our backs, yet as I listened to the list, there was nothing I wanted to leave behind. Lesson number one about camping . . . there is a huge difference between being comfortable and roughing it. Although I thought roughing it was exciting and what I wanted to experience, this city boy quickly realized that marshmallows and hot dogs were a great side dish compared to fish.

As dawn broke, we packed up everything, loaded it into one stuffed car and one loaded pickup truck and headed off to the jumping-off landing where we would pick up our one 16 and two 18 foot canoes. The Boundary Waters area is an immense landscape with over a thousand lakes, some large, some small, and very few of them connected by water. If you want to travel deeply into wilderness, a good compass, local knowledge and well annotated maps are critical. Since GPS did not yet exist, there was still this mystique about venturing out into the vast unknown. The other basic factor to be considered was portaging. The only method to get from one lake to another was to unload the canoes, strap on the backpacks, pick up your canoes and trudge to the next lake. Then you reloaded the canoes and started paddling again, breathing just a bit heavier. This process often constrained just how far one could travel straight north or any other direction in a given day. How much could you carry on your backs? How much difference did a foot or two of canoe length translate into pounds, especially after your third or fourth portage of the day?

Absolutely none of these thoughts had entered my mind before we did our first portage. We had been paddling for only two hours and with zero wind and mirror-like waters when we made it to our first portage. It was less than a hundred yards from our lake to the next one but the task of unloading the packs, strapping them on our backs, tramping a hundred yards to the next lakeshore and repacking all the canoes was like real work. Everybody carried

Lesson Seven

backpacks but Pa and Uncle Matt and Aunt Jo also hefted the canoes on their shoulders as well. My baby brother, Tom, carried a tiny fifteen-pound pack while I had a forty-pounder on my back. Even on that short portage I was envying Tom's light load. Our cousin Ronny, being in his later teens, carried a large standard heavy pack like the adults, but never got tired regardless of the distance. I was jealous of him as well. While that first portage was short, Uncle Matt said we had three more to go to get to our destination campsite that he had chosen, so we needed to step up the pace a bit to get there before dark.

In the middle of the afternoon we arrived at our final portage before reaching our campsite. There were a few groans from me and Tom but Ma pointedly reminded everyone that this was Roger's idea. And now he was whining! It got a good laugh and a couple of "serves you right" as we took on the longest and most difficult of our four portages. This one stretched for half a mile, but toward the end there was a large hill. Although not steep going up, it quickly got steeper coming down the backside. When we reached the top, we all paused and admired the view that overlooked a large deep blue span of water glowing in the late afternoon sun. Aunt Jo stretched her arm out and pointed to the far side and explained that was our campsite.

Seeing the end of our journey buoyed everyone as we started down the hill to the lake. Being a tad overexcited about the magnificent view and the thought of getting this heavy load off my back for the last time,

I took off with more verve than warranted by the topography to lead the group down the hill. Just a hundred yards from the lakeshore, the steepest portion of the hill caught me by surprise. Gaining speed as I neared the bottom, my toe caught in a tree root and I dove headfirst down the last steep portion, skidding the last half dozen yards on my belly and face down, driven by the forty-pound backpack. As I lay there stunned, wondering what happened, I heard lots of yelling and tramping feet, canoes being tossed on the ground as everyone ran to gather around the kid not moving. It was only a few seconds before I began to roll over and my mother reached me first. She was kneeling down with two hands on the backpack and all I could hear was her loudly proclaiming, "Oh my God, oh my God! His backpack! He has all the eggs in his backpack!"

Twenty minutes later, enough mercurochrome and bandages over my face to resemble a bad horror movie, all I could think of was that my mother was more worried about a few dozen eggs than she was about her elder son lying face down at the bottom of a cliff! We easily made it to the campsite situated on a real cliff overlooking the lake. The good news was I was exempt from any of the small chores I would have normally been assigned, like collecting firewood or cleaning pots and pans.

As the bandages came off, revealing scabs and a face that looked far worse than the actual damage caused by my headfirst dive, I took to sitting off to the far side of the campsite by myself pouting about the unfairness of life. I could not swim because the scratches, scabs and abrasions were still painful, but worst of all, my own mother didn't care about me more than those darn eggs! None of which, by the way, had broken. I did garner some respect and much kidding for skidding down the hill on my belly, thereby preserving many mornings of tasty breakfasts. It was during one of those pouty solitary sits when Pa came over and sat down next to me. As we looked out over the lake, we watched a solitary Loon and he said nothing for several minutes.

    Then he put his arm around me and quietly said, "As you grow up, you are going to run into this often in your life. Women are far more complex than you or me. She may have said something about the eggs, but she was in tears about you. You scared the bejeezus out of her with that tumble. Never ever assume what a woman says is how she feels. If you do, you will be wrong ninety times out of a hundred." It took me far too many years to remember and act on those words. Now, after three-quarters of a century, I'm still working on it.

Lesson Eight
Womanhood Deserves Civility

Pa displaying his life-long concern to protect Ma

One and Done

I HAVE BEEN CALLED a "loner" repeatedly in my life. It is the one trait that mystifies me in light of my parents' sociable habits. During my childhood years, folks were always stopping in to say hello, join us for dinner, or have a drink with my parents in the rec room down in our basement. As I think back over those years, I wonder when Ma and Pa had any time at all to themselves. Not that I ever complained, because every day brought new revelations, being near adults and hearing grown-up talk. It was a time of innocence that may be gone forever in our current society. A time of innocence that precluded general rudeness and four-letter words. In fact, throughout his life, I never heard my father use a four-letter word in front of my mother. And a muttered "damn" is the strongest I ever heard from him personally. While drinking in a tavern at the tender age of seven or eight, I first encountered this gentlemanly trait held so dear by father.

For several years, Friday evening was grocery shopping night at my mother's favorite butcher shop across town. I willingly tagged along, not for the shopping, but for the event that followed. (I was going regardless, because babysitters were not in the budget so it was simply whether or not I was going to put up a fuss.) After shopping, we would regularly stop at a nearby tavern that sponsored Fire Department baseball teams that Pa played on with his firemen buddies.

Milwaukee in those years was very much a "neighborhood bar" kind of city. Small corner taverns became nearly private social clubs for locals. You knew everybody and everybody knew you. It was "Cheers" except it was real life. Frank Fectow's bar was a firemen's hangout and for me it was always an exciting couple of hours listening to my father's buddies rehash the previous week's triumphs and disasters answering the fire alarms. Women's talk held little interest for me because Pa and his pals were hero figures in my mind, who ran into burning buildings to save people every day they went to work.

Exciting as the firehouse stories were, the best part was my role in the evening's festivities. When we arrived and all the mandatory backslapping and handshakes had taken place as we walked the length of the bar, Pa would find a barstool for Ma and stand next to her. He would then reach down, grab me under my armpits and effortlessly heave me up so I could sit on the edge of the bar between him and Ma. This usually brought cheers from the men standing next to us and I sheepishly had to refuse the raucous offers for a "boilermaker." A shot of brandy and a tap beer was known as a "boilermaker" and was the local favorite for most of the men in this milieu. Mr. Fectow, the bar owner would immediately place a small glass of Coke in my hand and the evening was off to a great start.

This child was fascinated to watch the way a group of larger than life heroes would interact as they unwound stressful workdays with tall tales and laughter among their friends and families. Now and again, strangers would walk into the bar, but they were always greeted cordially with smiles and nods even if they were not firemen. The good times and cheer were infectious and even strangers would soon feel like regulars. Often, they would join in what became a running gag at the bar. Someone would distract Ma and Pa and then one of the guys or Mr. Fectow himself would surreptitiously slip me some forbidden goodie. I was under strict orders to not ask for or accept any gifts. The gift might have been a small chocolate bar, a little chunk of salami or even one of those unnaturally red cherries that Mr. Fectow speared on a toothpick and drowned in one of the wives' drinks, but they were all off limits to me. Nevertheless, I was in an adventurous heaven with the deception, swallowing faster than I could chew just so Ma or Pa would not see my bulging cheeks. It was definitely a high point of those Friday nights.

The evening the giant came into the bar, I did not notice him at first. The giant and his two friends ended up standing just a few feet away from Pa where a couple of barstools had been empty. My father was a big man, standing six foot three, with muscles in places I would only dream of in my later years, but the man just a few feet away was a full head taller than Pa. I stole looks trying not to stare at the biggest man I had ever encountered in my short life. All three of the men were loud and seemed to be in a race to see who could drink the most in the shortest period of time. As succeeding boilermakers emptied and were refilled, the three, each in his own way, became louder. The big man with his back to Pa and the rest of us started arguing with his friend, while the third man tried to quiet them and defuse the argument without success. The giant began yelling as a result. They were using words I neither understood nor recognized. I could not even understand what the argument was about, but that it *was* an argument even I could readily grasp.

People yell for all sorts of reasons and under all sorts of conditions. Ma would yell at me when I left my bike in the driveway. Pa yelled at me when I did not put the lid back on the garbage can in the back of the garage. Both of them yelled for me when dinner was ready on the table, and I was a couple of houses away having lost track of the time. But yelling in serious anger is different and quite distinctive. The words have a harsh edge to them, usually accompanied by unnatural facial contortions and body language. Angry yelling is a flashing danger sign. It is a reliable warning that a decision point will soon arrive. A point at which one will be faced with choosing a path that will *always* have consequences. To determine exactly what those consequences are, good or bad, is a crucial life skill not everyone has the opportunity to hone or the smarts to remember. If one is lucky, one will have parents who preach and teach the law of consequences to you from a young age onward. It starts with small things, like after the third time in a row I leave my bike in the driveway, I will not be able to ride it for the rest of the week. That is a consequence that hits home for a youngster. Hopefully, as the consequences become more consequential in our lives, we will have gained the depth of experience necessary to readily assess and make reasonable choices based on those thoughtful assessments.

As the argument at the tavern grew louder and more heated, the rest of the patrons began to take notice. At the point when the giant nearly screamed out another word I had never heard before, starting with "mother—," the bar suddenly silenced. My father turned toward the man and gently tapped him on the shoulder. The giant spun around and, looking down at Pa, said in his still angry voice, "What the fuck do you want?"

"Look friend, I just want to remind you that this is a family place and there are women and children here. It's no place for that kind of language. Please fellow, take it easy. Cool down," Pa said in a very soft, calm voice with a big smile on his face. The entire place was now dead silent with every eye in the tavern focused on the two men standing toe to toe, one towering over the other.

"Mind your own fucking business," the giant said, as he started to turn back to his two companions. Pa tapped him on the shoulder again and the giant stopped turning and leaned down to Pa's face. "What now, asshole?"

"Listen I'm trying to be friendly here. Please do not use that kind of language in front of my wife and son and the rest of the folks in here."

"Fuck off," the giant said, staring down at Pa.

In a very low voice, almost a whisper, Pa said, "I am not going to tell you again. Shut it."

The giant straightened up, laughingly sneered and spit out, "And what the fuck are you going to do about it, asshole?"

I cannot relate what happened next because it happened too fast to be sure. My Pa flashed his fist a straight shot right up to the man's jaw and for a second or two, the giant's eyes unfocused and then he slid to the floor in slow motion. The entire room was so silent I could swear I heard his huge metal belt buckle strike the floor.

Pa looked at the two companions and said, "Pick up your friend and leave. Don't come back."

One of the men stammered, "I'll just pay the tab . . . "

"No, I'll pay your tab. You just pick up your friend and get out of here. Teach your pal some manners around women next time."

The two men grabbed their friend and dragged him out the door as Pa turned to me and Ma and asked if I wanted a hot dog, just as if nothing had happened. Instantly the raucous din returned with noisy laughter permeating the room as all the guys starting slapping Pa on the back.

I am fully cognizant this could never happen today. I am aware this kind of action no longer takes place without somebody pulling out a gun, but as I related earlier, this was a different time with different standards of civil discourse. As I grew up, I tried with some success to carry on that trait of oral civility my father held so dear, but I fear I faltered badly in later years. I learned all the words I had never heard in my childhood while I worked second shift in a machine shop, paying for my college days. However, I never uttered a foul word around my mother once, for the rest of our time together.

Lesson Nine
Man Up Even If You're a Woman

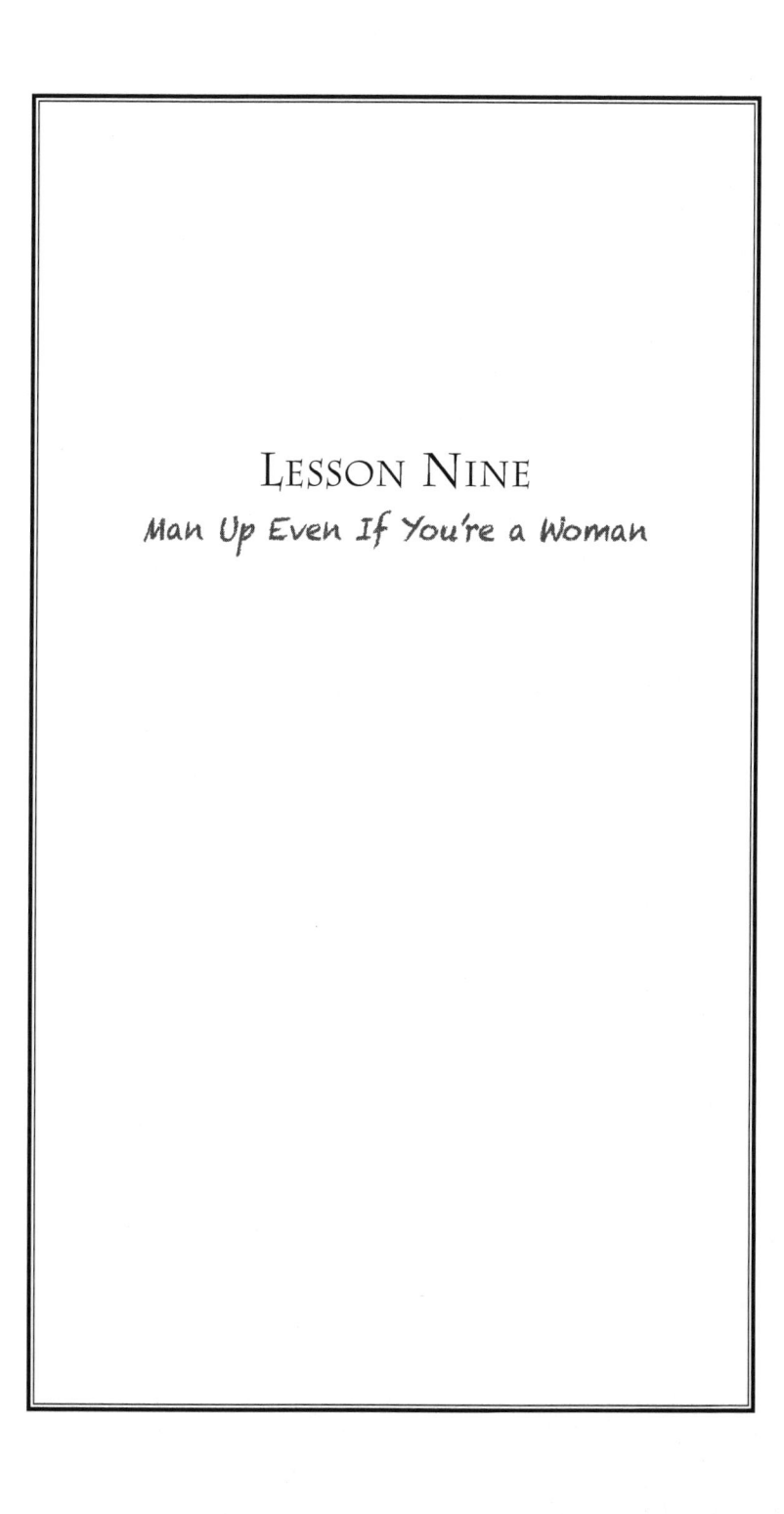

*Ma never flinched from challenges . . .
or responsibility*

Provo Promises

I HAD AN AUNT (one of my mother's eight sisters) and an uncle who lived in the glamorous and exotic city of Los Angeles, California. Twice, our summer family vacation was a cross-country road trip, camping out in the national parks there and back, but balanced in the middle by the miraculous sight of avocados, oranges, and lemons growing on trees in my Uncle Jack's back yard. As much as my kid brother and I enjoyed staying in the land of perpetual summer, the car rides through so many states whose names I only knew from pouring over the geography atlases in our house was the stuff of preteen adventure. To match the passing road signs with names on a map was fascinating to me and if my brother or I were sleeping in the back seat, Ma or Pa would yell out as we crossed another state line. High adventure for us Midwestern kids born in flyover country. One of those adventures occurred in Provo, Utah, a place and name forever etched in my ken. It was my first remembered exposure to deep and disturbing mortal fear.

It was a different time, and still a man's world on the surface. I would much later figure out that Ma ruled our roost, but superficially Pa was the titular head of our family. That meant the driver of our family car was nearly always Pa. But as for most blue-collar working men of the time, yearly vacations were only a two-week affair. Being a fireman with some seniority, Pa was usually able to get a few extra days added on for our cross-country road trips but still, a return to work was demanded on a certain day. Sometimes that meant long hours in the car to stay on a schedule that would return us to Milwaukee so Pa could report to the fire station on time. That also meant that occasionally Ma would drive while Pa nodded off for a few moments respite in the front passenger seat. Although I never once felt unsafe with Ma driving (after all, didn't all adults drive?) it was apparent to me that Pa seemed to sleep with one eye open whenever Ma was at the wheel.

On the day that perseveres in my memory, Pa had been driving since before dawn on our way back east toward Wisconsin. We had stopped along the roadside late in the afternoon for sandwiches that Ma had prepared the night before. She asked Pa if he wanted a rest for an hour or two while she drove. Pa agreed and we all piled back into the car, my brother and I in the back seat to watch for "padiddles." A "padiddle" was a passing car that had only one working headlight. Rarely seen today with the advances in technology, but in my youth a burned-out headlight was a fairly common sight. Spotting the car before my brother and claiming it provided one of the myriads of backseat competitions that eased the boredom of long car rides pre-electronic hand-helds. With the sun falling, we entered a construction zone just outside Provo, Utah. Blowing dust from road equipment billowed up around us as the '54 Buick

Lesson Nine

Roadmaster sped onto a rough patch of road surface. The rumble and vibration of the washboard road woke Pa, and as he rubbed his eyes, he opened them to see . . . nothing! The dust clouds had enveloped our car and the entire roadway while the setting sun, low on the western horizon lit up the dust cloud, obscuring visibility. Yet Ma did not hit the brakes or even slow down and flew blindly into the thickening cloud of dust. Pa sat straight up and yelled for her to slow down, but before he could finish the warning, a stupendous metallic crash sounded, lifting the fat old Buick up a foot or two before dropping it back to the pavement. The Buick came to a stop with the engine making strange noises.

    As the dust cloud dissipated, we could see we had left the road and were sitting twenty feet or so from the pavement. We had missed the slight bend in the road and crossed over into the construction area. There were no other cars in sight and whatever it was we had hit, it was not another vehicle. Ma sat with her head in her hands while Pa turned back to my brother and me and asked if we were all right. We were, but terrified would more accurately describe our state of mind. I was shaking and my brother was starting to cry. Pa then turned to Ma and in a harsh voice we had never heard him use before when he was talking to Ma, demanded, "My God! What were you thinking, driving into that cloud of dust?"

    Before she could answer, Pa was out the door and looking around at the car and the surrounding ground. He motioned for her to turn off the engine, which now was producing steam from under the hood. Ma got out and stood next to Pa. The air became still as both the wind and the dust dissipated, leaving us with a silent solitary vehicle sitting in the middle of a Utah wasteland.

    Luckily for us, several hundred yards away stood the field construction office trailer and even more fortunate, the door opened and a man in construction overalls and a hardhat came running over to our now silently steaming Buick. Pa and the man got down on their hands and knees and looked under our car, got up and walked to the rear and stood pointing and talking. Ma simply stood in front of the grille with her arms crossed over her chest looking forlorn and saying, over and over again, "I'm so sorry. I'm sorry. It was all my fault!" We had struck a basketball-size rock right in the center of the automatic transmission housing that caused the housing to crack and lose the fluid.

    The next three days were a trip highlight for my brother and me since we spent every available daylight hour in the motel pool while we waited for the replacement part to be installed. A luxury for us, because normally we camped out in National Parks on our road trips to save money. I did notice that Ma and Pa were noticibly subdued and I was sure it was not only about money but the fact that these three days meant Pa might not be back in time to report to the firehouse. He had never missed a day of work in all the years he had spent as a fireman for the city. I knew it was a matter of honor not only for him, but a trait instilled in his entire post WWII generation.

Lesson Nine

So, the night the garage called to say our car was ready and we could pick it up, we all celebrated by going to a local Chinese restaurant. That was another rare treat since we rarely ate out at restaurants, instead stopping at roadside pull-offs and enjoying pb&j sandwiches made the previous night. Pa quietly explained to my brother and me that in order for him to be in time to report for work, we would now have to drive nearly nonstop to get to our home still 1500 miles away. Since this was before the Interstate System was complete, many of those miles were on two- or three-lane highways that passed through small towns with stop signs and even a few stoplights. We were warned there would be no whining or unnecessary stops for any of us.

With the sun just brightening the sky behind the mountains to the east, we loaded the car and I watched as Ma walked toward the passenger side door. Pa said, "Wait Honey, you drive until noon, and I'll take over then."

Ma stopped in her tracks, looked at Pa, and then asked, "Are you sure you want me to drive after I made such a bad mistake the last time?"

"Sweetheart, you made a little mistake. O.K., maybe bigger than "little," but no one got hurt. It could have been so much worse."

"But it was so expensive. I don't know how we're going . . . "

At that point Pa put his arms around Ma and hugged her. "It's just money. We'll find it somehow. Let's get going. You drive first. We have a long way to go today." Then he hugged her for a long time and she got behind the wheel and Pa climbed into the passenger seat. I thought I saw a tear in her eye but she never looked back at us in the backseat so I can't be sure about that.

Many years later Pa and I were sitting on his pier fishing one evening and I asked if he remembered those eventful few days in Provo, Utah.

"Like it was yesterday," he said.

"Outside of the moment before you jumped out of the car, you never got mad at Ma the whole time. And then you let her drive the first thing after the car got repaired! Weren't you scared to let her drive again?"

"Of course, I was nervous about it but it would have been much worse for her if I showed that I was scared. She knew she had screwed up and she didn't need me to remind her of that. People make mistakes and you can always tell if they've learned something from them. Yeah, I think taking responsibility for what you do is probably the toughest job you'll ever have in this life."

As I think back on that serene moment on the pier with the frogs croaking all around us and the lonesome call of the loon echoing across the water of our bay just as the sun descended behind the White Oak trees around us, I fervently wished I had listened more carefully to his words. Maybe it would have prevented a few bad decisions and subsequent problems on my part over the intervening years.

Lesson Ten
Fear Does Not Make Cowards

*The ceiling stain never came out,
but only Pa and I noticed*

Better Living Through Chemistry

OK, I WILL ADMIT it openly. I am addicted to YouTube. Oh, not for all the weird stuff one is able to waste away hours viewing, but for the absolute breadth of how-to knowledge displayed on every imaginable subject. You can watch a video on how to do anything, whether it is launching your own weather balloon or how to grow rutabagas in your living room. I am also reasonably sure everyone has at one time or another clicked on a link they had not intended and got hooked watching a totally inane crazy video. A while back, that happened to me, and this particular video documented in dramatic fashion numerous episodes of dropping Mentos into a Diet Coke can or bottle and then running like the wind to evade the explosive results.

At first, fascinated by the visuals, I wanted to know why it occurred. Once I got the gist of the chemical reaction I sat back and began to reminisce about my youthful obsession with blowing stuff up. Firecrackers embedded in plastic toys large and small was my go-to favorite but secrecy was always paramount because hoarding the Fourth of July supplies had to be done surreptitiously or my career in explosives would have ended immediately when Ma or Pa found out. The saving grace was, as a young precocious preteen, I read everything and anything regarding chemistry. This fact was duly noted in our household and so as to encourage their son to become the next chemistry genius, one year I was given a large full home laboratory chemistry set as a Christmas present. I was beside myself imagining new excursions into destruction.

    That same winter, Pa had spent many hours and many dollars to reinvent our basement rec room for the family. He built a bar that could seat half a dozen adults, a back bar with a dazzling display of fancy glass bottles with exotic liquors like rum and bourbon and whiskey, all backlit and reflecting in the strategically placed shelf mirrors. I watched as Pa carefully and expertly placed tiles on the polished cement floor with nary a gap between any of the tiles. He installed knotty pine paneling along all the walls to a height of four feet and built false picture window frames above the paneling to imitate an above ground vista. Within the frames he seamlessly pasted photo murals of famous national park scenes we had visited during our summer vacations. In the center of the large room he spent an entire afternoon leveling our pool table, testing after each minute adjustment by rolling a pool ball slowly from end to end and noting any deviance from a perfect trajectory.

    The evolution of a dank and dark basement into this bright and welcoming party space took months and my brother and I were enthralled as we watched the breath of construction knowledge our pa had stored away in his head. As much as we enjoyed watching (and supposedly learning) these house transformation skills, the *pièce de resistance* was the ceiling. It was also the most complex part of the transformation. Before the time you could hang a metal framework and drop in ceiling panels, a false ceiling was a work of art. You first had to construct a lattice work of one-by-two wooden slats across the entire ceiling area and ensure that it was level front to back and side to side. To do this over an area thirty feet wide and forty feet long was a challenging project all by itself. Then placing the recessed lighting units and connecting them with the wiring was exceedingly time consuming. Once all was set and level, individual 12 inch square interlocking tiles with small perforations for sound adsorption were individually placed and stapled permanently to the wooden slats over the entire ceiling. Pa spent days and days putting in place the individual tiles and stapling the fitted edges so that no gaps occurred and the entire area would appear as one even, seamless white sky.

My brother and I were in awe, but also took great pride in the end result of those months of painstaking detail work. It was also apparent to us that Pa was pleased when Ma announced she was so excited about the new room, we'd host a neighborhood party to celebrate the completion of the rec room. My brother and I had seen other neighbors' rec rooms and none of them could boast a perfectly flat ceiling! In fact, most of them undulated across the ceiling above you like waves on the lake on a windy day.

This spectacular room was our new indoor play space for my brother and me and with still several days before the party, he and I began to load up the room with our favorite toys. He piled one dump truck after another throughout the area, but my exciting new chemistry set was front and center on my list of important installations in the new toy room.

Being the budding chemical genius I believed I was at eleven years old, I instinctively recognized that, careful as one may be, stuff spills. Working on the pool table because it was exactly the correct and convenient height for me, I pondered what might happen if I accidently spilled something on the perfectly level, bright green felt surface. There would be no safe hiding place for me if the unimaginable happened. But geniuses become famous for solving problems and I intended to follow in their footsteps. *This* genius solved his potential problem by spreading a large bath towel across the pool table top. Bingo, disaster averted even if something did go wrong.

Hubris is a wondrous trait. Completely obscuring reality, fostering a sense of personal euphoria as one blithely slides along living in a seemingly perfect world . . . until that perfect world collapses. No, I did not accidently knock over a test tube or tip a beaker with liquid. Nor did I set the basement on fire with a carelessly placed Bunsen burner. What I did do was mix enough different and cool sounding samples of chemical compounds that I had never used before. I also had not explored the properties of said compounds, but was sure they would prove an interesting experiment.

Lesson Ten

Soon the beaker of liquid began to hiss and fizz and I sensed a breakthrough. Being just slightly concerned about spillage and overflow, I doubled the towel around the beaker and put a cork in its neck. Again, a genius at work doing his thing, solving problems. Apparently, the hiss and fizz caught my brother's attention as well, and he ambled over to see what was happening. The two of us bent down with arms on the edge of the table and rested our chins on our hands intently staring at the now roiling contents of the clear glass beaker with the brownish bubbles blooming inside.

When the inevitable occurred, it was almost anticlimactic. There were no loud bangs or flashes of light or any noticeable explosions. The brown bubbles just continued to grow, when suddenly the cork popped off the beaker and a stream of brown sludge shot out of the neck reaching up, up, up . . . until it flattened out against the pure white ceiling tiles above it and slowly dripped back down to the towel covering the pool table top. It instantly stained the towel and saturated it, regardless of my ambitious attempt to catch the drips with my hands. My brother merely stood back looking up with a shocked expression on his face, while I could not take my eyes off the brown towel.

Of course, my futile attempts to clean this disastrous mess were less than adequate and the resulting brown stain on the ceiling was greatly enlarged once I had spread the spot by trying to rub it off with a wet rag. The pool table top responded to cleaning a bit better but one could still wonder if that slightly darker area was an overhead lighting shadow or an actual stain. Worse, there was a brown stain on my hands that did not respond to numerous scrubbings with Boraxo.

Swearing my brother to secrecy when Ma got home from work later that afternoon, I sat down on the floor looking up at the brown spot on the ceiling and I could easily make out a huge sneering smile looking back down at me. I logically assessed my options. The chance that Ma might come downstairs to the rec room after work was remote, so I had that going for me. In the immediate aftermath I was ecstatic that Pa was working that day and would not be home until the following morning. It would give me time to formulate a plan of action that might mitigate my impending death.

Alas, there were no revelations forthcoming and as the hours ticked by, I came to realize a very sobering fact. Anticipation is a two-edged sword. My destiny in the coming morning's confrontation was not only inevitable, it was going to be catastrophic. And I had many, many hours ahead of me to anticipate that destiny.

Vince Lombardi preached to his championship teams that fatigue makes cowards of us all. By morning, I knew the ambiguity of that statement. Sure, I was tired and fatigued because I could not sleep worrying about Pa's arrival, but my cowardliness was due not to one or the other but to equal parts of fear *and* fatigue. When Pa arrived home, I cowardly decided

I would wait until after his breakfast before telling him about the basement room. And then I cowardly delayed telling him while he and Ma talked about the preparations for the party in a couple of days. And then before I could tell him, he got up and went downstairs to check the beer supply. I sat as if I were nailed to the kitchen chair. The explosion I had not heard the day before, I certainly heard now. The rest of the day was not pretty.

My punishment contained the best of the hits from my previous transgressions and a few new ones. Although I am sure he was tempted far more times than I could imagine, I cannot recall a single instance growing up of Pa striking me in anger as a punishment. I did have cousins who were noticeably bruised upon occasion. I would pose that bruises disappear in a few days but losing an entire summer's worth of swim time or biking excursions with buddies was just as painful and just as long lasting sociologically. Ma's admonishment throughout that summer echoes within me yet.

"You know your father loves you, but you made everything so much worse by not telling him what you did immediately. That was the part that made him so angry. How many times has he said to you that being afraid of the truth is worse that the truth itself?" I did remember hearing those very words from him. Sad to say, there have been times when my memory has failed me regarding that sage advice.

So chemistry had not made my life better at that point and to this very day, with the exception of some medical breakthroughs for which I am grateful, I am not convinced of the efficacy of that corporate tag line that was so prevalent in my youth. Better living through chemistry? Hmmm, perhaps, and perhaps not.

Lesson Eleven
Anger Clouds Judgement

Site of the long-deceased temporary trailer

Rattling Roofs

My folks retired to a finger of land jutting out into Wisconsin's best walleye lake. It was raw land when my father bought it, but being the quintessential handyman, he planned to build for my mother her retirement castle on that finger of land. While the construction of this home was in progress, they lived in a small house trailer temporarily placed 20 yards away but still close to the lake. In an effort to make the temporary trailer more comfortable, my father and I one weekend built a deck and enclosed it with screens and a roof so my mother could sit and watch the progress of her dream house arising on that point of land jutting out into the lake. Pa and I positioned eight of the 4 x 8 foot sheets of corrugated aluminum up on the roof but only minimally tacked them down so they would not slide off. Since it was getting dark, I decided we were done for the day, regardless that I got the stink eye from Pa who would have gladly continued the job right through the night given his personal work ethic. However, in deference to his bossy son, we sat down to enjoy the evening sounds in our newly enclosed veranda that effectively doubled the size of my mother's temporary living space.

It will come as no surprise to those who knew me then that I had the unenviable trait of impatience.

Nothing could happen fast enough for me. Coupled with what would be a life-long tendency toward procrastination, I would often be gently chided by Pa about this incongruity in my makeup.

"You want everyone else to hurry, but are never in a hurry to do your own part," was a refrain I heard often while growing up. Now, as a young married man, I still had not learned the lesson. My wife at the time, however, was a taskmaster for any and all projects concerning me. So, when I stopped the roofing process by putting in a few holding tacks as darkness began to fall, my wife made a point to mention that I could have put a lantern out there and finished the job before we quit for the night.

I got just a bit ticked (OK, maybe some real anger crept into my tone) and said, "Not only is there no real reason to go up on a slippery aluminum roof in the dark, you were not the one working all day long to build the two-by-four and two-by-six framework. I'm tired and want a beer. The roof will still be there in the morning." Anger always obliterates patience and harsh words nearly always negate tolerance. It is a bitter lesson, difficult to absorb, particularly when you believe you are in the right.

I knew Pa was just as tired as I was, and that cold beer refreshed both of us as we admired a good day's work. The new structure was solid and extended the full length of the thirty-foot house trailer, almost doubling the floor space. We had also temporarily tacked up the screening on the sides to assure we could survive the mosquito attack that occurred every dusk in this part of the north woods.

Lesson Eleven

With a cold beer in hand, the Schlitz label clearly illuminated by a shining half-moon and stunningly brilliant Milky Way above us, this city dweller sat transfixed by a starry night sky that extended right to the horizon, sharply defined and undiminished by any light pollution. As one beer turned into two, neither Pa nor I noticed the growing void rising on the western horizon, blacking out the starshine with a distinct but foreboding harsh line.

A hard day's work well done is a mesmerizing event. While we all relish the end of the day's labor, (except for my Pa perhaps) we also tend to black out the myriad of normal daytime musings. That often includes our personal observational skills. When Pa rose out of his chair and started to tidy up, I told him to go to bed because I would clean up and bring in the empties before I retired for the night. Not quite ready for bed, I was reluctant to end the personal high of the day's accomplishments. Sitting alone while the half-moon's shimmering reflection on the water highlighted the gently swaying cattails lining the shore, I watched our local beaver swim directly through that moon's reflection to the far shore across the bay. Now, tired and lubricated by a couple of beers, I got up and went into the trailer, totally neglecting to pick up the folding chairs or the empty beer bottles scattered about our new porch.

A little after midnight, with all of us soundly asleep, a distant rumbling signaled one of those summer thunder storms that periodically blow through the upper Midwest during the warm months of June through September. Of course, it woke my wife, who was terrified of thunder, and who in return woke me to tell me it was going to storm. Still irritated by her pointing out my earlier display of laziness, I shushed her in no uncertain terms and told her to go back to sleep. Besides, although I felt confidently expert at anything and everything in those years, I did recognize that my control of the weather was somewhat limited. After all, summer rainstorms are brief and renewing. Let it rain and thunder. I could sleep through almost anything.

Almost anything. A crackling, ripping crash, a thunderous boom, and a screaming wife will do it every time. Stumbling into jeans and a tee shirt, I rushed out to our new porch and turned on the big yard light. Drenching rain and whipping winds had bent over every tree in sight and I could not grasp why the new porch was all wet and rain poured over the upturned chairs I had left sitting in the middle of the new floor. As I stared at the sight half asleep, trying to make sense of what I was seeing, Pa shoved me aside as he went through the doorway out into the maelstrom. Now fully awake, I followed him out and we were both completely soaked instantly.

Thunder boomed in a continuous rumbling; lightning flashed with only an instant of dark intervals making the yard light totally unnecessary. Looking up into the driving rain, it was obvious that three of the eight 4 x 8 aluminum roof sheets were missing and the rest, held only by a few tacks, were noisily flapping and dangerously loose during the wind gusts.

Lesson Eleven

Pa immediately spotted the three missing sheets ten yards away, all bent and threatening to end up in the lake with the next blast of wind. He yelled at me over the din to help him and we charged after them before they could disappear into the lake and be gone forever.

Carrying the three sheets back to the trailer, we secured them by tossing them under the deck and put the upturned chairs over them to weigh them down. I grabbed the ladder and put it up against the porch structure while Pa got the hammers and nails, then I climbed the ladder and sat astride the nearest open roof beam to nail down the remaining roof sheets. It was then I realized, Pa was wearing shoes! He was smart enough to recognize they might be useful. That would explain his being behind me getting to the door as we came out. I was still barefooted!

True to form, the winds moderated as did the drenching rain while Pa and I nailed down the roof sheeting we should have secured earlier in the evening if it had not been for my laziness. After an hour or so, we had completed the task under the dim glow of a yard light, getting no help from the bright moonlight still blacked out by the retreating storm clouds. It was a tired and wet pair of men who climbed down from the porch roof at four in the morning, no longer concerned about storms and rattling roofs.

That should have been the end to a trying episode but as often occurs in life, challenging events tend to cascade, one after the other. After putting away the ladder, feeling pretty good about meeting the crisis, but completely ignoring that I was the cause of it to begin with, I strolled under the newly secured roof admiring our handiwork. Ma was pouring a freshly brewed cup of coffee inside the trailer for all of us, but I was looking up and smiling. That's when I felt the stabbing, sharp pain in my right foot. Looking down, I saw that a broken beer bottle was slowly turning a bright shade of red. Blood red. My blood, to be exact. Just a small reminder that I would not get away scot-free for my hubris in allowing laziness to stoke my anger and setting in motion events that would ruin a good night's sleep. In retrospect, I was correct about the roof "being there in the morning!" However, on the negative side, it is incredibly embarrassing to apologize to a wife after she has uttered those damning words, "I told you so!"

Lesson Twelve
Justice CAN Be Swift

Deer hunting is a religion in Wisconsin

Fountain City Bluff

The Mississippi River took a few hundred thousand years to carve its way between Wisconsin and Minnesota, leaving along its banks a sometimes rocky and sometimes tree covered bluff varying in height from fifty to several hundred feet in some areas. Meandering first near and then away from the river's current bed, the bluffs are unlike most of the rest of either state where rolling hills, interspersed with lakes and farms, are the more common landscape features. Because the bluffs were too steep for farming and too unstable for houses, they evolved into a natural undeveloped playground for nearly all wildlife indigenous to the upper Midwest. These bluffs were particularly suited to the plentiful white-tailed deer who can romp up and down the steep bluffs with seemingly little effort. Hunting deer in bluff country requires the legs of a lion and the lungs of an elephant. Far more male egos are shot than deer in that compact but rugged ecosystem.

    I was fourteen the first time Pa and I went to the western edge of the state to hunt the bluff country with my cousins from the dairy farm. Cousin Bob's wife Rhoda had family just above Fountain City and their farms along the Mississippi River on the Wisconsin side included some of the highest and most rugged bluffs in the entire river watershed. It was unlike anything I had ever hunted before in my brief woodsman career. In fact, this would be the first time I had hunted anywhere but on my Uncle Roy's farm in central Wisconsin.

    The topography of the central portion of Wisconsin is gently rolling hills interspersed with patches of hardwood and pine forests, separated by plowed or fallow farm fields all atop a sandy loam soil base. It is an ideal spot to use a technique known as the "controlled drive" method of deer hunting. Simply put, one would station several of the hunting party at one end of a patch of forest and several others would drive the game to the standers from the far side. Although this sounds unfair to the deer, in reality, stationing three or four hunters across a half mile of forest edge was often less than effective. Deer are smart and cagey about where to sprint across open spaces and many a deer, I'm sure, has laughed as they bounded away between two hunters a few hundred yards apart who had never looked in their direction at the crucial moment.

    So bluff country would be a new experience for me, and although the morning rituals were the same, rising well before dawn, eating a big breakfast, then shivering with the first few gulps of icy air in the below-freezing temperatures of the predawn, I was nervous. I needn't have been. Our hosts were gracious and the two families merged easily into a group of ten or twelve men playing out the age-old role of hunter-gatherers. As the youngest, I was exceedingly proud to be accepted and included. Another manhood milestone reached!

Lesson Twelve

I quickly learned the most difficult lesson in hunting bluff country. One drove the deer not up nor down the bluffs, but rather across. This meant one walked with one leg uphill and one leg downhill. And on those steep grades, it often meant one foot was continually ten inches above the other. Think about walking along steps one foot always two steps above the other. The uphill leg gets pretty tired and exposes any weakness in the knee or thigh. Now I understood why us youngsters did the driving and the older men did the standing.

It made no difference to me, however, as I reveled in the outdoors, and at one particular moment was able to look out through a break in the heavily forested bluff and see the fabled Mississippi river below me. Little patches of snow along the river's edge and a mirror of ice on a pond here and there sparkled at me in the crisp morning sunlight. From this height the river looked smaller than I had expected, but as I watched, a tug made its way slowly upriver, appearing as a mere toy in the wide expanse of steaming water. Now the river's breadth looked huge.

The morning went quickly with little to show for our efforts. No one had seen, much less, shot at a deer. Because it was opening day of the season, we expected to have more opportunity to spot deer than later in the week when deer would become more wary of the intrusive and dangerous noise from hunters. We ate lunch slightly disheartened but confident the afternoon would bring a change of luck.

I was midway down a bluff traversing it when up near the high side of the bluff I heard yelling and two shots rang out. My cousins were above me with Pa below me but I thought I had recognized Bob's voice, though I was unable to catch his actual words. It is uncommon for the drivers to see the deer. They normally keep well ahead of the approaching hunters but apparently one had attempted to sneak back between us and had been spotted. Our luck had changed!

When Pa and I arrived at the scene, it was obvious Cousin Bob was having quiet, but nevertheless strong words with his younger brother, Rolly. As we were able to piece together the gist of the story, it appeared that Bob had yelled to Rolly that there was a small deer coming his way, but to let it go by because it was too small. Rolly either had not heard him or chose to ignore him and had shot the small deer, which looked barely larger than a big dog. Bob was incensed that we should waste a buck tag on such a small specimen that would yield so little meat after it was dressed out. Rolly was just as adamant that they keep it because it was his first deer after several consecutive and embarrassingly dry hunting seasons. They reached a compromise.

We would field dress and drag the small deer up about fifty more yards to a small tractor road cut into the hill and finish the drive we all had started. Then we would obtain a doe tag (none of us had one on us) and come back for Rolly's little deer. It seemed to solve several issues . . . we had to finish the drive, (the standers would be waiting for us), Rolly would get to keep his first deer in several years, and Bob would be happy to not use up a buck tag on this pitifully small deer. Bob rapidly field dressed the deer and we placed a few branches over the carcass just off the dirt pathway. We then rather quickly finished our drive, meeting up with the standers, and told them about the deer a mile or so back down the hill.

With nothing to do until Bob and Rolly returned with the deer, Pa, myself, and my third cousin Dave decided to walk along and accompany them instead of simply waiting at the cars for them to return. Although the mood was a bit strained, Bob still being ticked at the waste of a tag regardless that it was a only a doe tag. We all were in good spirits because one of Bob's in-laws and the owner of the land we were hunting on, Merlie, had shot a nice eight point buck on our drive. The easy camaraderie of the men around me made it short work of the mile hike we had to get back to the spot where we'd left the deer.

As we turned the last little bend in the path, a hundred yards up ahead we saw a Jeep parked very near to where our deer was hidden. Immediately, Rolly sprinted ahead of us to investigate. Pa, sensing something amiss, grabbed my arm as I attempted to run ahead with Rolly. Pa simply said, "Slow down, stay with me until we see what's up."

By the time we walked the last hundred yards to the Jeep, Rolly was yelling at two hunters we did not recognize. They were yelling at him. And everybody was yelling loudly. I heard Bob murmur under his breath, "Oh no . . . damn!" And he picked up his pace, as did Dave and Pa and me.

    At this point I should perhaps mention briefly my three farm cousins. All three were much older than me, but I saw them as role models. Bob, the oldest, was probably in his early thirties at the time and married to this beautiful girl with the strange name, Rhoda. He was the most entrepreneurial of the three; while outwardly always calm, composed and unflappable, there seemed a sadness deep down inside I wouldn't be able to account for until much later in my life. Dave, the middle cousin, was an easygoing guy who gave me his .22 to use when we came across the cottonmouth snakes in the swamp, let me drive the tractor before I was legal, and showed me how to handmilk the cows. Rolly, the youngest of the three, was a short, fiery hothead, a wild and crazy guy who thought he was James Dean. Rolly wore his emotions on his rolled up tee shirt sleeve, right next to the pack of Lucky Strikes and dared you to make something of it. He also took me for dusty, fast rides on the back of his Harley hog over the bumps and ruts of the dirt roads in the back forty. It was only with white knuckles that I managed to hold on, all the time thinking at any moment I would fly off into space and land in a cornfield or on a rock pile. Pa never knew, Rolly never told, and I idolized him for giving me those adrenalin rushes. And they all called my Uncle Roy "Pa." It is where I got the handle for my own father and ever since have used the same appellation. Pa — it just seemed right then and it still feels right today.

Lesson Twelve

When the four of us came on the scene at the Jeep, the dynamics suddenly changed. Rolly, undaunted by the fact he was outnumbered, was beside himself in spite of the presence of the two big guys with guns on both sides of him. When they saw us approach, they both stepped back from Rolly, allowing us an unimpeded view of the Jeep. Tied across one of the fenders of the Jeep was Rolly's small dog of a deer. It had a deer tag on it.

In Wisconsin, hunting is a religion. And deer hunting is fundamentalist religion. The rules are many and inviolate. Always ask permission to hunt on private property and always respect other hunters in the field are only two of a myriad of tenets every boy learns by heart as he grows into his hunting manhood. Now here were two men who were on Merlie's property without permission, and what's more, they had put a tag on a deer they had not shot! This was an unheard of breach of ethics and something I could not have conceived of ever happening.

Worse, here was Rolly yelling, the two men yelling back, insults flying back and forth and getting more and more vile. We watched as Bob rushed up to step between them before Rolly shot someone. A scenario that didn't seem all that unlikely to me, by the way. Calm and collected, Bob tried to reason the facts out, but the reality was that a tag was on the little deer and it was not ours. The only way we were going to get that deer back and legally register it was to cut off their tag. It would mean a completely wasted tag to the two hunters, something they were not keen to give up. As I edged closer to the action, both Dave and my father grabbed my arms and held me back. Pa said there were already enough people in the immediate vicinity of that Jeep. In fact, they both stepped back a bit with me firmly held in their grip. I did notice they both held their shotguns in a relaxed but convenient grip. This was high drama and I was a witness! Maybe even a combatant. It would be another ten years before I truly understood what horrendous damage guns could inflict.

    We three were now about 20 feet from the front of the Jeep where the other four were still arguing. We could easily overhear Rolly and the two strangers, but Bob, as was his nature, spoke slowly and quietly and we had to listen carefully to understand his words. He listened as the men explained how they had thought the deer had been abandoned. They had no response as to why they thought a dressed out deer had been abandoned. Rolly yelled out again that they were nothing but a couple of rotten poachers. They bristled and hands gripped shotgun stocks more tightly. Bob suddenly yelled out to us, "Uncle Bud!" (although my father's name was Raymond, everyone always called him Bud). Pa looked at Dave and a look passed between them and Dave squeezed my arm tighter as Pa walked up to the Jeep. He and Bob had a few quiet words with the two men while Rolly tried to worm his way between them but was elbowed out by Pa and Bob. Then Pa calmly walked back to where Dave and I stood and simply turned as we waited for the drama at the Jeep to play itself out.

Lesson Twelve

I expected more fireworks with Rolly being as hot-headed as he was, but to my surprise, Bob stood in front of Rolly and said, "O.K., enough. We're not going to kill each other over an undersized deer. Rolly, we're going to let them have it. And that's the end of it." Rolly fumed but Bob's force of character won out and Rolly, although he continued to mutter to himself, started to back off. He was turned toward us, but over his shoulder yelled back at the two strangers, "You think you pulled a fast one and got away with it, but there will be a come-uppance. Mark my words. Justice will prevail." He walked over and stood next to us, still fuming. Meanwhile, Bob turned and faced the two men and quietly said, "Get in your Jeep, take the deer and get out of here. Don't ever let us find you on our land again." They did as they were told, unloading their guns before putting them in the back of the Jeep. Visibly relieved, they slipped into the front seats while Bob stood directly in front of the Jeep still with a menacing look on his face. It was obvious emotions were running high on all sides but the tension definitely lessened as Bob finally began to turn and walk back to where we were all standing.

Then, without any warning, Bob turned back to the hunters now seated in their Jeep, and said in a voice louder than I was accustomed to hearing from him, "And just so you remember that you've made a mistake you shouldn't make again . . . " with one arm he suddenly aimed his shotgun down at the radiator of the Jeep, which was no more than three feet away from him . . . and pulled the trigger.

I visibly jumped at the loud hollow blast of the 12 gauge shotgun and the slug hitting the metal radiator instantaneously.

A 12 gauge shotgun slug used in deer hunting is slightly less than the size and thickness of a man's thumb. It makes a large hole in whatever it strikes. In the case of the Jeep's radiator, the fluid gushing out was like a small green river. In the aftermath of the blast echoes, no one moved. The two strangers were frozen to their seats, Rolly's eyes were smiling and Bob looked extremely grim. Pa and Dave once again grabbed my arms and roughly started me off the path and down into the forest. Rolly and Bob were right behind us and we all easily disappeared into the underbrush.

It would be a long walk out for the two men in the Jeep, an expensive tow back to a garage and all for a very few tiny venison steaks. I will forever remember Pa's words to Bob after we got a ways down the hill. He put his arm around Bob's shoulder and we all heard him say in that raspy but clear voice of his, "Yup, sometimes justice comes quicker than you'd expect." We all laughed loudly, but mostly I think it was out of tension relief.

Although in my later years I would come to honestly believe that a gun was rarely a solution to anything, I would forevermore envy the swift and sure justice of that old Remington Model 10 twelve gauge shotgun.

Lesson Thirteen
Don't Assume You Know People

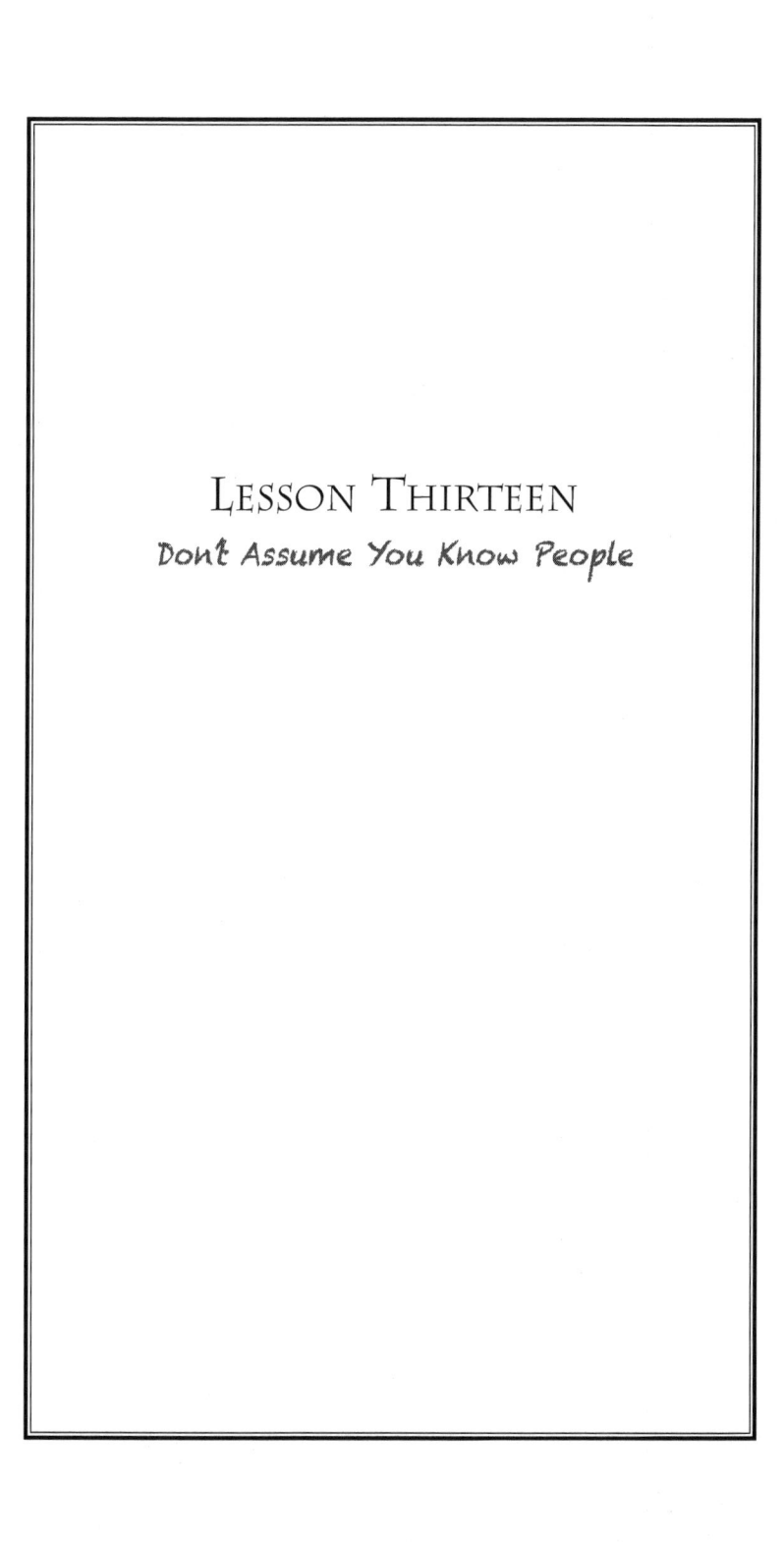

There are surprising facets to a man's strength

Sad Sacks

My FATHER HAD RETIRED, so in my myopic view, I considered him to be an old man as he entered his middle 50s. But in deference to respect, I asked him if he would help me move my business to a new location. My business involved the processing and duplicating of motion pictures and necessitated keeping supplies of chemicals used in the process. With myself, my brother, and my three employees, my father joined us in lugging equipment and film stocks out of the low two-story building into the rented truck for transporting to the new single-level location. As young bucks in their 20s and 30s are wont to do, we made light of the "old man" and repeatedly teased him, telling him to take it easy and let us do the real work. Just how irritating that can be was driven home to me only recently as my now 40-something son refused to let me help him move some heavy furniture.

On moving day, we enjoyed a beautiful fall crispness with cool temperatures and sunny skies that produced smiles and energy all around. The heavy equipment had already been moved by professionals and we were loading up the small stuff that didn't need lifts, dollies and strapping webs. After clearing the first floor and returning with the truck we knew the tough part lay ahead of us. The basement area is where we did processing, mixed chemicals and stored raw materials. One of those raw materials was a chemical we bought in granular form packed in eighty-five pound sacks. We bought that raw material by the truckload and still had more than seventy sacks to carry upstairs and load into the truck.

One of the Foolish Five, as we would later refer to ourselves, suggested a challenge. All of us not yet in our thirties, we felt ready for any dare. Who could carry the most heavy sacks up the twenty steps from the basement and load them into the truck? Deciding on the stakes took a few minutes, with no small amount of braggadocio being displayed by me, my younger brother and the three young bucks who worked for me. I agreed to buy lunches for a month for the winner but also suggested the worst of us Foolish Five would have to perform end of day cleanup at the lab for that same month. Incentives working both sides of the aisle, as they say.

Normally we were each assigned one day a week (including myself, boss or no boss) to perform one of the more onerous jobs at the lab. Once we all had shaken hands on the deal, we all started hedging toward the door, no one wanting to be the first one to break ranks and run to get the jump on the others. As we looked at each other warily, Pa quietly stepped in front of us and said in that whispery, smoke-damaged voice of his, "What about me?"

"What about you?" I asked, perplexed. Surely, he did not intend to carry these eighty-five pound sacks up those stairs? He was old! He'd kill himself!

Lesson Thirteen

"Don't I get to get in on the action too?"

At this point my three young employees tittered but my brother stayed silent and said nothing. I was not paying a great deal of attention and simply said, "Pa, these sacks weigh eighty-five pounds. Way too heavy for you. Stay in the truck and stack them as we bring them up to you."

"Well, I think I should be allowed to compete as well, even if I am decrepit." He did have a small smile on his face.

"Well . . . sure . . . O.K. . . . I guess. If you really want to . . . " I stammered.

"Wait a minute," Jimmy, one of my employees butted in, "When he comes in last, he won't have to clean the lab for a month cuz he doesn't work here! That ain't fair either."

Pa smiled at Jimmy and said, "How about if I come in last, I buy you ALL lunch for a month?"

There ensued several loud comments all at the same time ranging from an enthusiastic "Yeah!" to a subdued, "Don't want your Dad to hurt himself."

Now, feeling a bit guilty about it on several levels, I looked at Pa and asked, "Are you sure you want to do this? These things are really heavy."

His only comment?

"Yeah, I think you mentioned that already. We can stand around here all day and argue about this or we can get the job done. Which is it going to be?"

At that, everybody took off for the basement. We all lined up respectfully in front of Pa and picked up a bag and started up the stairs. We were putting each of our bags on the hydraulic tailgate lift when Pa appeared at the doorway and walked over to us. He was carrying one sack ON EACH SHOULDER!

"Hey," one of the young employees said, "That's cheating."

"Didn't hear nuthin' in the rules about carrying only one sack," Pa said, with a huge smile on his face.

We nearly ran to the basement now that we were all down one sack in the count. Carrying two sacks however was a tad more difficult than we had anticipated. I simply could not get that second sack up on my available shoulder. Nor my brother, nor two of the three young guys. The third young man, Robert, a weightlifter, managed to get two up but he was staggering side to side as he slowly made his way up the stairs. The rest of us decided speed would win the day for us and we took only one sack but leapt two steps at a time going up the stairs.

The day wore on and what started out as a lark competition for all of us became darn hard work and tiring as well. We had become seriously "sad sacks." It is a shameful trademark of youth to grossly underestimate the time and effort required to accomplish even the most menial of tasks. All of us learned a lesson or two that day. Mine was somewhat akin to that of the old lawyer's admonishment to "never ask a question you do not already know the answer to." In my case, it was to "never assume you have the measure of someone just because you know them."

In the greater scheme of things, it is not only embarrassing to be out-muscled, but out-maneuvered

Lesson Thirteen

and out-thought as well, is particularly galling. Pa did us all in that day as we wore ourselves out trying to catch up to him in sacks carried. He didn't carry two sacks every trip but as soon as we narrowed the gap a bit, he would pop up the stairs with two sacks, one on each shoulder again, widening the spread to a comfortable lead over his young competition. By the end of the day, we youngsters could barely walk while the "old man" quietly asked if we had any more bags to carry. My brother, of course, related the entire day's antics to our mom, who merely smiled but said nothing.

A few years later I would be sitting at their kitchen table looking out over the northern Wisconsin lake where they lived and I asked Ma if she remembered that iconic story about Pa and his Herculean strength as told to her by my brother.

"Of course. How could I forget it? It certainly was not the first story of its kind that I had heard or witnessed. You know, don't you, that he carried every single bag of cement down from the road we used to mix and pour the concrete floor in the basement when the cement trucks wouldn't come down our little driveway? So your father just carried down a hundred or more of those bags to mix by hand. If you are ever lucky enough to be married to your best friend," (I was NOT at the time), "you will always remember with great pride those incidents that define your partner. Your father never mentioned to me personally that incident when he helped with your laboratory move, but I could tell something happened that day that made him smile inside. Those moments of quiet pleasure you sense in your partner? Well, they stick out in your mind like a flashing beacon. Quite nice, actually!"

And she took another sip of her famously weak coffee, looked out over the lake to the opposite shore where a family of geese swam in a meandering conga line. I knew she was in another place altogether. A place probably further away than I could imagine. I could, however, judge it was far distant by the gleam in her eye and the small smile on her lips.

Lesson Fourteen
Loyalty Is Manliness

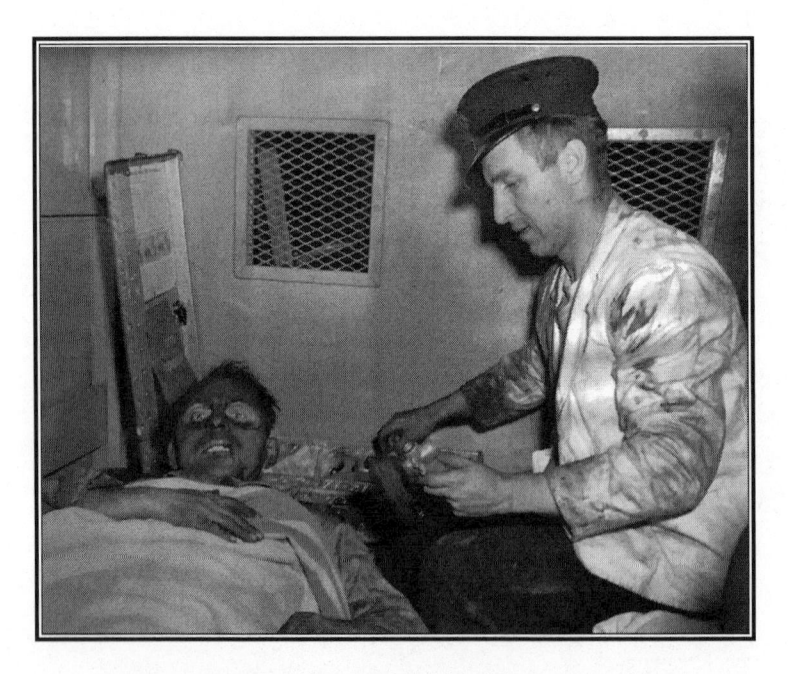

Pa treating a fire victim in the city's first Rescue Squad vehicle

Hero-maker Haymaker

IN MY YOUTH it was still fashionable to look up to firemen as heroes and that was exactly how my brother and I saw our father. But my mother also thought of him in that light as evidenced by the large scrapbook she secreted away from him but which contained all the clippings of the fires he worked and especially pictures from the newspapers in which he could be identified. One memorable moment occurred when we received a long-distance phone call (a rarity in our household), from my Aunt Helen in Los Angeles. She had been reading the morning edition of her *Los Angeles Times* and noticed a picture of a large burning building in Milwaukee. There was a long ladder from a hook-and-ladder firetruck extended way out over the roof of the blaze, and at the very top was a single fireman with a hose spraying water down onto the roof of that huge blazing building. My aunt said to Ma, "I suppose that crazy fireman at the top of the ladder out over the fire was your crazy husband, wasn't it?" Ma looked at Pa and smiled a little and said, "Yes, it was." Ma may have been proud of her "crazy husband" but certainly no more so than the pride I felt all the time I was growing up.

But the one photo of Pa that always comes to mind was one showing a black-sooted and smudged fireman dragging one man and carrying another out of a smoke and fire-choked storefront building. Heroic as it looked, it was merely the aftermath of truly heroic action I would never have known about had I not been sneaking a few moments eavesdropping on one of Pa's fireman gatherings in our basement rec room.

Our basement rec room (built by Pa) was little different from every other basement in the neighbors' homes in our working class neighborhood. The rooms pretty much mirrored one another with knotty pine paneling, suspended ceilings, tiled floors, a pool table that doubled as a ping pong table and, of course, the bar. Our rec room was the social focal point for not only neighbors and friends but also other firemen who would stop by to jaw with Pa about something, usually asking him to help them with a project of some sort. Every now and again, the rec room party was almost exclusively for firemen. Perhaps it was a retirement or a promotion for one of the men, but those parties always ended up loud and produced a copious number of empty bottles, both beer and liquor. Something else came out of those parties — stories. Story upon story of derring-do and screwups and bad bosses and the worst fires.

Early in any evening my brother and I were relegated to the upstairs but as the evening went on, nobody cared about the two kids sneaking down the stairs and huddling near the open doorway, taking in the yelling, laughter and back-slapping among the men crowding around the small bar. By the time our bedtime rolled around my brother and I were invisible to the entire crowd. The stories got longer, the laughter

Lesson Fourteen

got louder and the cigarette smoke thicker. When Pa finally noticed me, he merely held out his arm and without a word, pointed for me to go upstairs. He did not have to say a word, because I knew my time was up. My brother had already gone upstairs and I turned to follow him. But several of the men had turned back to see where Pa had been pointing and they saw me. One of Pa's best friends yelled out to me, "Hey, Kiddo, come over here."

He always called me that. I hated it. I was torn between minding Pa or entering into the inner sanctum as commanded. When a couple of the other guys also called out for me to come in, I sheepishly walked down and over to the bar. The group made a small space for the skinny eleven-year-old at the bar and Pa's friend Sam (not his real name) put his arm around my shoulders conspiratorially and pointed to Pa with his other.

"Kiddo, do you know your old man is a hero? Do you realize he is bravest man in the entire city fire department? He's done what all of us really have wanted to do for years. But your old man did it. And do you wanna know what he did?"

Pa jumped in and again pointed to the door while he quietly said, "I think it is your bedtime, Roger." I started to pull away from Sam's bear hug but he would not let me go.

"Oh, c'mon Ray," Sam said, "let the boy hear this. It's a story he's gonna hear sooner or later anyway, and besides, it's gonna make you famous."

"Not even close, Sam, just let it rest."

Then, almost to a man, the others chimed in and yelled out, "Tell it Sam, tell the kid the real story."

Sam looked at me and asked, "Did you see the picture in the paper of that fireman carrying one guy out on his shoulder, while with the other arm he was dragging a second fireman out of the burning building?"

"Yeah, Ma said it was Pa."

"Well, Kiddo, I was the guy he was dragging out by the collar of my firecoat. And I got the bruises to prove it. Yup, that was your old man being a hero but that ain't the whole story by a long shot."

"Really, Sam we don't have to go into this. The boy should be going to bed," Pa said, trying to head off the story before it got good.

"No way, Ray," one of the other men said, "he should hear this."

"Yeah, Bud, let him be. Sam, tell him the real story. The best part of the story." Pa was called Bud as often as he was by his real name, Ray. The six or seven men around the bar got quiet as Sam smiled and said, "Well, you know I can't speak to that part. I was inside that damn firetrap of a building trying like hell to not get killed when the roof started to cave in."

One of the other men jumped in and loudly proclaimed, "Hey, I was there. I saw and heard the whole thing, start to finish. That old four-story was blazing from the basement through every floor right to the roof. No way we were going to save it. We got the call to evac and we all hopped to it and skedaddled out as fast as we could."

Lesson Fourteen

Sam interrupted him and "NO, not everybody. Almost everybody got out, but me and Jerry, we didn't hear the recall signal. We were way in the back of that first floor and we didn't hear nuthin but the roarin' flames around us."

And then a third man spoke up, "That's when it got interesting cuz we were all standing outside countin' noses. The Big Chief was right there with us because his office is right up the block. Someone, I don't know who, yelled out that we were short two guys."

And a fourth guy at the bar chimed in yelling, "And that's when Bud yells out, 'Where's Sam and Jerry?' And we all look around and sure enough, Sam and Jerry aren't with us. Somebody says they saw them head to the back of the first floor to seal off the basement passage." Looking directly at me he points and says, "And that's when your old man starts to put his helmet back on and yells out, 'we got to get them out of there. That roof's not going to last long.' But the Chief grabs your old man's arm and won't let it go. 'No one is going back in that building — it's too dangerous. That's why I called for the evac. Stand down, Raymond.' The Big Chief, he knows your dad, cuz' him and your Dad, they got a history. But that's a whole 'nother story."

"So what happened?" I ask.

"I'll tell you what happened. The Chief is hanging on to Bud's arm and your Dad says, 'Let me go. We gotta get our guys out of there.' The Chief says 'Nobody is going back in there. Besides, they can get out the back.' And your old man jerks his arm away from the Chief and says. "They'd have to jump in the river to get out and if they did they'd drown with all the equipment they're wearing. I'm going back in. . . . ' The Chief grabs Bud again and says, 'Over my dead body. I said no one is going back in there and I mean it.' And that's when your old man hauls off and decks the Chief. Right on the jaw and lays him flat on the ground — the Chief of the whole department! He slugs him and runs right back into that blazing first floor."

And yet another of the men at the bar gets into it and says, "But that ain't all. That skinny little photographer from the morning paper? Can't remember his name but he's at every call we get downtown, he's standing right next to me and sees the whole thing coming down. So what does he do? He puts up that big old camera of his with the flash bulbs and just as Ray slugs the chief, *BAM*, that flash goes off. Sure would love to see THAT picture in the paper."

"And if you did, Bud here would be out of a job for sure," Sam retorts. "So the picture of your father carrying Jerry and hauling me out of that hellhole is the picture the paper prints. Lucky for your old man, Kiddo, or else you'd have to get a job! They couldn't fire a hero after that picture was on the front page of the morning newspaper."

They all laugh and start jawing at one another while Pa opens up a few more bottles of beer and with a cross look at me points to the doorway and I hotfoot it upstairs. A couple of weeks later a large

Lesson Fourteen

envelope arrived at the house addressed to Ma. That "skinny photographer" included a short note with an 8 x 10 black and white photo of a fireman swinging a right cross at the head of the Chief of the city Fire Department. His note merely said, "This is buried in our archives, but you should get to see it. Your husband is not only a hero, but his loyalty to his buddies is a thing that makes legends." Ma showed it to me and my brother but when Pa saw it, he got kind of strange about it, grabbing it from Ma, and simply saying, "Loyalty is more important than any old job." I never saw that photo again although I have looked through hundreds of old black and white photos that Ma left in boxes. What I did find was the simple truth. My father lived all of his 83 years by his own code of manliness.

Lesson Fifteen
It's Not Always Clear Cut

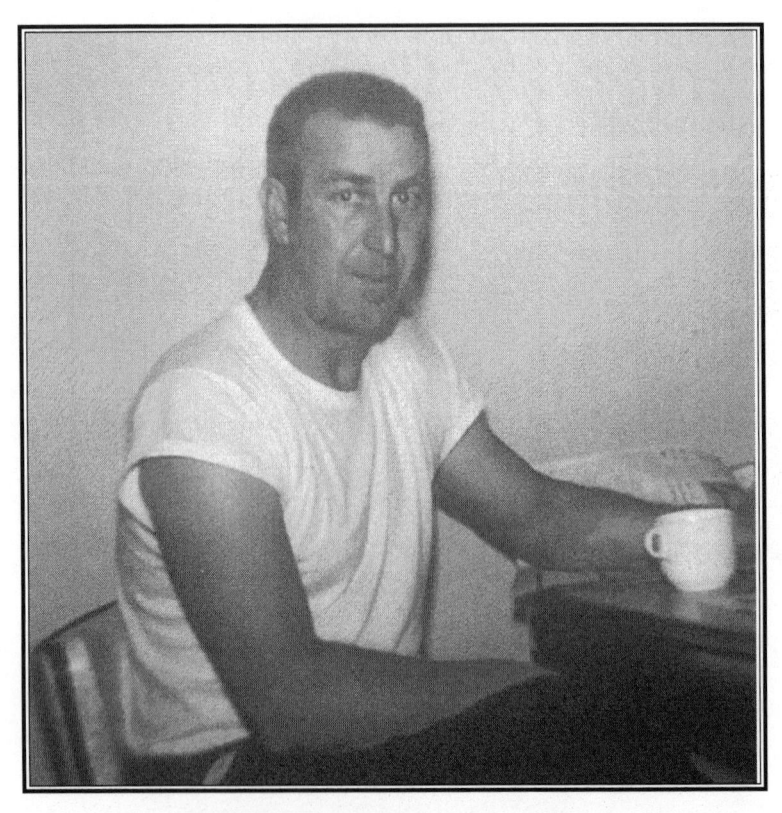

Indecision was rare for him, but he had difficulty with me this time

The Devil and the Deep Blue

IN THE SUMMER of my seventeenth year, my first year of college finished, I went to work for a large local manufacturing firm to earn enough for the next semester's tuition. Hired as a Process Laboratory Technician II (16 cents an hour better than a Tech I because of a chemistry course . . . education pays!) I was excited by the prospect of working in an actual laboratory. Of course, I had lied about my age, but in those days anybody who wanted to work could find a job, and besides, at six foot four I looked older. After all, lots of 21-year-olds had zits! Another factor adding to the anticipation was the opportunity to be independent of my folks, who were subsidizing my schooling and my life. Rightly so, they thought they should still have a say in my comportment and responsibilities around the house. I, of course, being 17 going on 30 felt I was now a man of the world, no longer subject to the yoke of childhood chores.

    I soon learned that the "researching new methods of manufacturing ferrite magnets" consisted of six or seven excruciatingly boring chemical tests, and many hours of equally mind-numbing grinding, pulverizing, and pumping of slurries composed of ferrite powders in mini-micron size. The ferrite powders, many times finer than face powder, came in three basic skin-staining colors. Perhaps staining is the wrong term. Because the individual particle sizes were so tiny you could place a teaspoonful on the jeans covering your thighs, gently tap your thigh with a finger next to the powder and it would sift through your jeans in a matter of seconds to wind up forever deeply embedded in the pores of your skin. Suffice to say that substantial and frequent scrubbing was necessary to expunge the telltale red or greenish hues, but it was a small price to pay for living the romantic life of a scientific researcher with a regular paycheck!

    The group I was a part of who led this process laboratory was an eclectic mix of college has-beens, wannabees, and never-woulds, all considerably older than myself, alll of whom further added to my sense of grown-upness. We worked, played softball and basketball, and drank together. In those days no one cared to check for fake IDs. It was my first experience in being part of a group. In school, I was always two or three years younger than my classmates and never fit in socially. My father's admonitions that when one runs with a crowd, one becomes the crowd never seemed to make sense to me because I never had a crowd with whom to run until now.

    One of the more interesting of my co-workers in the lab was a guy I called Cool Kenny. You know the type from every school class or work environment you've ever been in. . . . Mr. Cool has always just been to the best concert, has a stunning girlfriend, drives the fastest wheels and is never at a loss for words. And this particular Cool Kenny was everything I thought I wanted to be. And one more small detail.

Lesson Fifteen

As a side job, he owned and operated a skydiving school at one of our local private airfields in his off hours. He could go on for entire lunch hours with tales of daring-do floating through the clouds and soaring with the birds. I was mesmerized.

When I shyly asked about taking lessons from him he was, as expected, nonchalant and said, "Sure, come out to the field Saturday morning and you can sign the release forms." I was concerned about that "signing forms" business for just a moment, but the old saw about "in for a penny, in for a pound" seemed to make perfect sense to me and I promised myself Saturday could change my life. The thought that it could also end it never entered my ken. At age 17, all young men are immortal in their view of themselves and I was no different from any other foolish teenager.

I was up early Saturday morning, skipped breakfast and efficiently mowed our lawn because it was a Saturday chore I was expected to complete to pay in part for my room and board now that I was a paycheck-wielding corporate worker bee. A few eyebrows were raised since I rarely completed this chore without substantial prodding or direct threats. I also knew asking permission to do what I intended would be a fruitless endeavor in our household so one more piece of wisdom floated through my head. That would be the one about it being easier to ask forgiveness than to ask for permission, so secrecy would be my mandate for the immediate future.

I had never been to the small private airport 10 miles from our house. In fact, I had never been to any airport at all in my seventeen sheltered years of life. Of course, I had never been in an airplane in my life either. Now I was planning on taking my very first airplane flight — and then jumping out of the plane! But surely that would not be today since I needed to be trained and schooled in the intricacies of skydiving by Mr. Cool Kenny. There was no doubt in my mind however that I would be cloud-soaring soon.

Upon parking my 1955 VW bug on the gravel up against a rusted chain link fence a mere twenty yards from the only runway, I could see across an expansive green grass field. I opened the door and was assaulted by a roar so loud it shook the VW. A vintage single 16-cylinder rotary engine T-6 trainer sporting faded and peeling Army Air Force insignia clawed the air as it slowly gained a little altitude to clear another chain link fence at the end of the runway. Mesmerized by both the sound and the closeness to this airplane I had only seen in jerky documentary films at school, thoughts about my upcoming training were put out of my mind as I walked over to the Quonset hut that served as the airport's operations center.

Cool Kenny sat at a small desk in the corner and waved me over as he took out a sheaf of papers. His first words, "Didja bring the cash?" echoed in the empty room but never fazed me. I counted out the $75 and handed it to him. He pushed the sheaf of papers to me and said, "Fill these out while I go pay

Lesson Fifteen

for some gas." My first thought was, "He needed my $75 to buy gas? Does that mean he intends to fly today? On my money?"

"When I get back, we'll get you outfitted."

"What about my training?" I asked as he slammed the rickety screen door on his way out. He did not respond to my question. A few gray clouds drifted across my mind at that moment in time but the paperwork stared at me as I took up the only pencil in sight. The three or four pages of badly xeroxed and nearly unreadable forms delineated in a myriad of ways that Cool Kenny would not be responsible for anything that went wrong. Mentioned items included, but were not limited to "the airplane striking the ground with me in it," the "parachute not opening with me attached to it," and my favorite, "any or all injuries sustained by me for any reason whatsoever."

For the very first time in my weeklong odyssey of romantic anticipation leading up to this very minute, I suddenly realized there might, just might, be a downside to this exotic cloud soaring business. Nevertheless, I signed the three lines at the end of the last sheet of xeroxes, carefully lying again about my age and, perhaps the most thought-provoking, made up a name for next of kin in case the worst occurred. I did not have much time to parse the meaning of all this because he returned with an armful of strange looking equipment which included a football helmet.

We walked outside to a picnic table where he began to lay out the equipment on the table-top, leaving a corner of the edge uncovered. He looked me up and down, all skinny six foot plus of me, and asked if I needed to wear the glasses. I said I did.

"All right, stand up on that empty corner of the table," he ordered.

I did and felt a bit foolish standing up there looking down at him. He was starting to lose his hair on the crown of his head. I never noticed that before.

"O.K., this is how you are going to land when you get back down." Upon which he stood in front of me and twisted his knees a bit to the side and fell to the ground with the rolling taking up the brunt of his fall. "Now you do the same thing when you jump off the table. Remember to do the rolling bit like I just did."

I did it and he said it was O.K. but we needed to practice this important technique. It would prevent me from breaking an ankle or my leg or both of them. As he explained it, my jump off the table was similar to the force with which I would land with the parachute deployed above me. I did this jump from the picnic table about a dozen times and we moved on to the next phase of my training: which line to pull to control my direction while I was floating down. Left line to go left and right line to go right. Wow, very technical! Then he made me spread my legs and lean sort of spread eagle over the picnic table.

"This is the position you will take when you crawl out under the wing to stand on the wheel before you jump. Don't worry. We'll practice it before the plane takes off so you are comfortable with it.

Just remember we will be traveling about 80 or 90 miles an hour up there and the wind will be like trying to pull you off, so you have to make sure to hang on until you're ready to jump."

Next, he made me lie down on the grass on my stomach and then told me to lift up my arms and legs so I was only resting on my tummy. When I did that, he told me that was the position I would take immediately after leaving the airplane and before my parachute opened. Any other position would not be good when the parachute on my back opened. I took careful note of this crucial technique, my head swimming with all the new details necessary for cloud soaring. At this point, Cool Kenny made me stand up and started to fit me with the paraphernalia he had laid out on the picnic table. The very last piece was a bulbous fanny pack that attached to me in front and was connected to my parachute harness.

"This is your reserve chute," he said. "If for any reason the main chute does not open, you just pull this here big red ring and your reserve chute will come out. Got it?"

What? What if the main chute does not open? In a dense fog of TMI, I muttered yes; grabbing my arm, he walked me the fifty yards to a sleek red and white Cessna 182 reeking of gasoline fumes.

"Are we actually going up now?" I asked.

"Sure, I don't want you to forget what I've taught you," he replied.

"What about how I pull the ripcord on my main chute," I stammered.

"Your first few jumps will be with a static line attached to the plane. You don't have to do anything. It will pull your chute out when you jump."

With that, we got in the plane and he started it up. I was so enthralled about being in a real airplane I never thought much about the end game for my virgin flight. Excitement has the positive result of producing endorphins that mask and often obliterate dark thoughts of a possible reality. The plane ride was extraordinary, seeing our local town from a vantage point totally foreign to me was everything I had envisioned. In a flash it was over and within half an hour I had jumped out, floated down and landed uneventfully. The feelings were as advertised. It WAS like floating among the clouds (even if there were no clouds in this summer sky). No eagles checked me out and no curious birds flew past me but it was magical nonetheless.

Later that day when I arrived back home, I was so pumped I could not contain myself. I had jumped out of an airplane! I could not confide in Ma or Pa but maybe I could brag a little to my younger brother, Tommy. Under pain of death, I swore him to secrecy and blurted out what I had done. At first he did not believe me, but the Polaroid Cool Kenny had taken of me on the ground with the parachute spread out behind me and me with a grin extending all the way to Iowa was enough to convince him. I knew it would. What I didn't know was that my brother could never keep a secret. I learned that lesson at our family dinner that night when he practically screamed out, "Guess what Roger did today?" between scooping more potatoes on his plate.

That was my second lesson for that day. With the cat out of the bag, I excitedly related the day's events, skipping over the parts about lying and falsifying legal documents. I wanted to get the exciting and brave part out before the hammer fell. I knew Pa would go ballistic. However, once again, I was wrong. He sat at the dinner table with a fork and knife in his hand, unmoving. Not eating, not moving the food around on his plate, just staring at me with no discernable anger as I spun my tale.

Just as I was finishing my story, my aunt and uncle came in the back door to our kitchen to visit. They were invited to sit with us for dinner and my adventure was not brought up by anyone, including my brother, who now knew I was going to get him. Truth be known, the adventure was not brought up at all for years to come, much to my great surprise. No screaming by Pa, no punishments, no tears from Ma. It was like a non-event in our family.

I would look back and realize the position I had put Pa in that evening. On one hand, I had done a foolish thing, endangering myself and the happiness of our family; on the other hand, his son had jumped out of an airplane the very first time he had ever flown in one. Should he be proud? Should that small display of perceived bravery be lauded? Should the foolish decision making be punished? Should he be angry? Could he be both? Or could he be neither? I do not know how many other similar situations my father faced dealing with me, but this was certainly a difficult one. He was caught between the proverbial "devil and the deep blue sea" with this wayward son of his. I am not sure if he ever figured it out. I know I have not.

Lesson Sixteen
Stand Your Ground, But Know It First

*Pa's pier remained private property . . .
even if a VIP used it*

FISH OR CUT BAIT

MY FOLKS' RETIREMENT HOME sits astride the best walleye fishing lake in Wisconsin. In fact, my father's pier tickles the edge of the best "fishin' hole" on the entire lake. Unfortunately, this location is well known to many others also and opening day of walleye season is often a traffic jam of men and small boats jockeying for position 15 to 20 yards off my father's pier. This yearly event never seemed to irritate him; rather, he was greatly amused by the amateurs snagging their lures on nearby boats, shoreline trees, and each other. He would sit at the kitchen table with a cup of strong black coffee and watch out the large windows overlooking his point of land that jutted out into the lake and silently chuckle at the humorous scenarios being played out so close to his pier. My father never fished opening day but merely waited until the following day when the lake in front of the house was once again empty of everything but the fish.

His and my most memorable opening day was also the least crowded in his memory of over thirty years. In fact there was only one boat slowly moving to and fro over the vaunted "hole" in front of the pier. No doubt this dearth of action was due in no small part to the bone chilling dampness imparted by a 33 degree temperature and a nasty 18 knot wind blowing promises of snow and frostbite out of the northwest. That lone boat, however, carried the illustrious governor of our state, a man not held in much esteem by my father.

I, being in my teens, was quite impressed with the fact that such an important personage was right out in front of our home. My father simply reiterated his disdain for the Governor and justified his opinion by pointing out the fact that anyone with a brain would be drinking coffee in front of a warm fire waiting for the weather to change, not freezing his butt off while preparing to get soaked in the obviously fast approaching thunderstorms. Besides, real fisherman knew no self-respecting walleye was going to rise to the bait under these conditions anyway.

To their credit, the two men in the boat saw the same rapidly approaching squall and were already moving toward the safety of my father's pier. They had no sooner grabbed the pier and thrown a line around one of the bollocks to secure the boat when the squall hit. A mixture of sleet, snow and rain all swept across our point blurring out our view of the boat and the two men but we were able to discern that they had both gotten out of the boat and were huddled together on the bench we kept on the pier. As the wind and sleet lashed them and their boat my mother suggested to Pa that he go invite them in to the house. Pa replied that it wasn't necessary because he could already see the squall was passing and it was going to turn into a simple driving cold rain in a few minutes. Besides, they shouldn't have been out

Lesson Sixteen

there in the first place. They'd be safe enough for the next few minutes and then they could be on their way home if they had any sense at all.

Again, as he predicted, the sky brightened slightly, the wind dropped back down to a mere 15 knots and the sleet and snow turned to a heavy, cold drizzle, actually a respite from the previous ten minutes, and we fully expected to see the men climb back into their boat and resume whatever their plans were for the balance of opening day. But surprisingly, they did not climb into their boat but instead began to cast their lures into the lake, fishing nonchalantly from my father's pier.

Now, up in the North Country, original home of the Posse Comitatus, where nearly half the land is water and half the water is land, certain rules of etiquette prevail regarding fishing near or on private property. These rules are backed up by laws defined in the trespassing statutes. Anyone had the right to fish any portion of the water including up to the very edge of private shoreline, but one must do so while ON the water. Any foray on land requires permission from the landowner. And a pier is always considered an extension of the owner's property. Over the years, I can recall many times when fishermen would come to our door and ask permission to fish off our pier or shoreline and my father would always say yes, go right ahead. The really smart ones would leave a fish or a couple of bottles of beer on the porch as a thank you but they always had the courtesy to ask before venturing on to the private domain my mother had named Ramiroto Point.

And here were two men calmly casting lures from our pier and making no move at all to come up the thirty or so steps to our door and ask permission. The lights from our windows streaming out into the deep gray day were easily visible and advertised that somebody was inside, yet they made no effort in our direction. This was a major breach of etiquette, not only in my father's mind, but also in the mind of anyone who lived in the North Country. I could tell my father was not happy about this lack of manners. My mother and I could both feel the rising tension in him with every passing moment those two interlopers did not turn and walk towards our house and do the right thing.

"Pa, he's the GOVERNOR of the state," I offered softly.

"Who he is has nothing to do with WHAT he is doing. And what he is doing is trespassing without permission," my father replied in a quietly determined voice. "My taxes pay his salary and he's a powerful person in the State Capitol, but that doesn't give him the right to flaunt the law, son."

"Dear, it's no big deal. Besides, it's raining," my mother offered, knowing full well where all this was leading.

"It's raining on their boat as well as it is on my pier," my father quietly replied as he put on his rain slicker and moved toward the door. In a flash I had my raingear on and was out the door on his heels. I wasn't going to miss this for the world.

When we walked out onto the pier the man with the governor nodded to us and cast his lure into

Lesson Sixteen

the lake. My father calmly inquired as to what they were doing. The man said they were fishing. My father informed them they were on private property, at which point the first man gave an exasperated sigh and turned to my father and said, "Do you know who this is? This man is the GOVERNOR!"

"I know who he is, but you're both trespassing on my property." Again, my father's voice was hush quiet but his eyes were shards of flinty granite.

"I don't think you understand . . ."

"Oh, I understand perfectly. You are trespassing on my private property and I'm telling you to get off my pier. I don't care if you're the President. Get into your boat and off my pier . . . now." This all said in that quiet and calm voice I knew to be backed with steely resolve. To someone not familiar with my father, I am sure it sounded menacing in the extreme.

"Just who the hell do you think you're talk—," the man said with his voice raising.

"John, John, hold on here," the Governor interrupted, while stepping in front of the man and facing my father directly face to face. Actually he had to look up as my father was considerably taller than he was but the Governor did not seem at all intimidated. "This man is absolutely right. We're on his pier. And sir, I'd like to apologize for my friend's bad manners. Please accept our apologies."

With that, he nearly shoved the other man into their boat and pushed off from the dock. As the wind took the boat out from the shore, we could still hear the man protesting to the Governor, "But you're the

Governor . . . ," and the Governor holding up his hand to the man as if to say "enough, enough."

A few moments later, back in the house, I related every word to Ma while she brewed a new pot of coffee. All she said to me was, "Yes, certainly sounds like what your father would say."

At first, I was somewhat impressed with the Governor for standing up and taking responsibility for his careless actions. Something I felt no politician would do in this day and age. My father, however, simply said, "We've yet to see how honorable the governor is."

My father was correct to withhold judgment. For the next three years my father's state income tax returns were audited. Of course, he had nothing to hide and furthermore, he was also unperturbed about the frequent visitations in front of our pier by our local game warden. Being well known to us, he was too embarrassed by his "mandate from above" route and so I noticed he would always look out to the lake and not at our pier as he passed. And I'm sure he could say with an honest conscience that he had made another trip to check up on that troublemaker guy who lived on Ramiroto Point.

The only time my father ever mentioned the incident to me again was years later, and all he said was, "A good man will always stand his own ground. You just have to be sure you know the ground you're standing on." Easier said than done, but through the years, I've tried to remember that simple instruction.

Lesson Seventeen
There Is a Big Picture, and It Isn't Sex

Cousins played a large role in our growing-up times

Cousin Cuisine

My hormonal awakening, as unique and mysterious to me as it is to most boys, occupied not only my waking hours but most of my sleeping ones as well. It was my two slightly older girl cousins who brought the reality of my impending breakthrough to the attention of my parents, causing my father one of his rare moments of indecision regarding direct father-son intervention. I would learn of this indecision only much later, of course. By that I mean that my brother and I were always included in family activities but not as peers. Activities were for sharing among the family, each taking out what pertained to us as individuals. This selective adsorption worked on several levels and resulted in relatively little boredom among the members of our extended family that included my many cousins, of whom I counted nine in our city alone.

Around the age of ten or so I had two favorite cousins who were slightly older, but both girls were precocious and smarter than me. I was fascinated at how they would finish each other's sentences even though they were not sisters but merely cousins. As my first concerted interaction with girls, I was totally clueless, just as my male peers were at that age. After all, we had just come to the realization that girls were not like us. We had always known they did not like playing in a muddy sandbox, did not like baseball, did not like boys, and yet suddenly these horrible faults meant nothing to me. This revelation was difficult to assess for a ten-year-old.

Having cousins stay over for a night or two was common in our growing-up years. I would spend a night or two with Cousin Jack or Cousins Betty or Diane or Carol and their sisters and they would visit our home for "playdates," as they were called at the time. It would be many years later when I realized the playdates were actually baby-sitting efforts among our close-knit families. As kids, we all liked each other. We always enjoyed our times together whether they were spent at each other's houses or sleeping together in the haymow barn on the dairy farm owned by another aunt and uncle in the central part of our state.

The dynamics were changing for me, however. The girls seemed different. They continued to treat me the same as always, belittling boys in general, laughing at times when I could discern no reason for laughter, but with a subtle difference. They appeared to take more direct interest in whatever I was doing. In the past, as cousins, we always had fun but with a normal boy/girl separation. They played different games than we boys and yet there were always those joint endeavors that ended up in laughter and dirt smudges on faces. Normal stuff for young kids growing up in that 1950's postwar bubble. As for us boys, I do not think we had a clue that we were changing and growing up every day. I am pretty sure the girls were far more attuned to maturation issues affecting their daily life, their activities, their hormones, well before me and the boys.

The changes most clear to me occurred when Carol and Betty came to our house several times over that particular summer. They recruited me to be a patient while they played doctor. We would go off to one of the empty rooms in the house and they would order me to "be a good patient" and not complain about what I was told to do. They would be laughing and giggling at most any reaction I had to their instructions, but it was a new game and I liked being with my older cousins.

No, it was never about genitalia, but it was about hands-on touching. My ears closely looked into, or my chest listened to were the most regular inspections. At first, I was squirmy and a bit squeamish about why I had to do these things. They sternly rebuked me, and since I adored my smarter cousins, I ultimately submitted to their ministrations until that certain day. Because I was wearing a blindfold they had put on me, I did not see the cause of their sudden disappearance from our "examination room." All I knew was they had left the room and I was lying on the bed with a blindfold over my head in the middle of the day awaiting new instructions.

After a long time with no one answering my questions I gave up, pulled off the blindfold and sat up. Walking out to the kitchen, I asked Ma where the cousins had gone, and she simply said they had to go home early. For a long time after that I was quite aware that we had no more girl cousins sleeping over. Boy cousins, yes, girl cousins, no. I was perplexed, but most disturbing, I missed those "doctor sessions!" I had grown to enjoy the attention paid to me by the two girls and even their laughter at my squirming reticence. And now I missed them and their weird game!

It would not be long before the emergence of erections while thinking about the girls would lead to self-cognizance regarding girl cousin sleepovers, girl cousins, and girls in general. It would be far longer, in fact it would be a couple of decades before the curtain would be drawn back on those early "doctor" experiences. Fifteen or twenty of us first cousins were gathered for a family reunion when my cousin Betty came running up to me and jumped up to give me a big hug. This was not easy for her since she's well under five feet and I am 6-foot-4. She then turned to the other cousins around us and loudly proclaimed, "This is the first man I ever slept with!" That certainly quieted the crowd. A hushed silence was followed by a few interspersed "Whaaa's?" and a few more "Huh's." Betty was never a shrinking violet and she laughed conspiratorially and started in with the tale of her and Carol's "doctoring" Cousin Roger in the privacy of our bedrooms when we were children. I immediately jumped in to correct the impression I could tell was permeating the other cousins' thoughts.

"Wait, wait, wait, don't get too excited. It was never about sex. They never felt me up. They never

Lesson Seventeen

took my pants off!" At which point Betty punched me in the shoulder.

"You were so, so stupid, Roger. Of course, we intended to get your pants off. Carol and I both wanted to see for ourselves what you boys had that we didn't!"

"You what?" I blurted.

"And you are still stupid, apparently!" she laughed.

"When Aunt Dolly saw what we were doing that one day, she shooed us out in an instant," Carol chuckled. "Betty and I laughed all the way home!"

They always referred to my mother as "Aunt Dolly." Then I related how I lay on that bed with a blindfold on for what seemed to be an hour waiting for the two of them to come back. That got an even bigger laugh from the now rapt cousins. It was well over a year later when I confronted Ma in person about that episode. She smiled at me and said of course she knew what was going on.

"It was then I knew you were going to be just like your father. Even at only ten it was plain to me you would like girls. So I told your father what happened when he got home the next morning and he was in a quandary about what to do. We both wondered if he should talk to you about why the girls were no longer going to be sleeping over. But your father thought about it and finally decided we would let it pass. He said it was the big picture he was concerned about."

"The big picture?" I asked.

"Yes, your father said in the greater scheme of things, sex was not going to become more important or less important to you just because he broached the subject now or let nature take its course. He thought you'd have to come to grips with being a boy on your own. So we just never said anything about your cousins."

Now, after 75 years of living, I can look back and truthfully say that yes, sex was a big deal to me ever since those first awakenings. Of course, Pa was also right again. Although sex has been pretty damn important, it has never been the "big" picture of my life. However, I do believe Cousin Betty continues to think I am stupid.

Lesson Eighteen
Keep Both Eyes Open

*My longtime nightmare exactly.
Alas, this is a stock photo, the only one in the book.*
Photo credit: Byrdyak

Bear in Mind

The ethereal wilderness of my late teens, that time when I never recognized the trails that led one from childhood to adulthood, was matched by my fascination with an actual wilderness of trees, rivers, mountains and solitude. A form of wanderlust that would only grow with the years. I fervently sought out opportunities that would take me to the pathless vistas of Ketchican, Whitehorse, Sitka and the Yukon.

When my friend Larry asked if I would take over a pro gratis photo shoot of a grizzly bear hunt while he earned actual money for a paying job, I said where do I sign up? When I called Larry's friend, the hunting guide Rolf, to get details and times, I was surprised to learn our hunting party would be small. Besides Rolf and his old friend, Moresby, who doubled as cook and gunbearer, there would be only the hunter with the trophy tag — Rolf referred to him as "the Client" — and myself. I asked about my weight allowance and received a loud guffaw in response.

"Vell," he started, "you take vhat ebber you vant. Vee go in by boat and zen pack 12 kilometers to zee base camp. You must carry 10 kilo pack vee gif you and vhat ebber you vish to carry of your own, you can bring so long you carry yourself."

"We're not flying into your base camp?" I asked.

"No fly. River and svamp. No place enough vater to fly in. Must valk to base camp."

He gave me the time and place to meet the boat and I hung up. I had been to several Canadian and Alaskan hunting lodges and fishing camps in the past couple of years, but all had a lake big enough to land a small plane for easy in and out access. This seemed a bit more primitive. If we were being put ashore from a boat and packing into a river valley or delta, we must be looking for coastal bears. Duh, it struck me suddenly. A trophy bear! Of course! That would have to mean a coastal brown bear. They were always the biggest bears in Alaska because of their diet. Grizzlies, Alaskan Browns and Kodiaks are all the same bear genetically, the only difference between them is size and diet because of where they live. Bears inland on the tundra or forest had to work much harder to fill the protein larder than the island locked Kodiaks or coastal bears.

The Coastal Browns have the best cuisine of the three. Starting with salmon and plenty of it all spring and summer, they grow fat quickly with minimal effort. Even if their fishing skills are off kilter for a few days, the southern Alaskan coastal areas are lush with berries, grubs, and small animals. Or large animals . . . the Alaskan Browns are not choosy. These bears have no natural enemies in their kingdom except man. They rule their domain at a lumbering pace because they can. That is not to say they are not fast, they simply choose to saunter from meal to meal. That 1500 pound lumbering behemoth can reach speeds of 40 miles an hour! No doubt they revel in being king of the hill. Or the valley if it pleases them.

I was feeling excitement as I stepped onto the wet dock at the small fishing village in this quiet bay. My floatplane had skimmed onto the flat water of the bay after a two-hour early morning flight out of Vancouver, and from the air I had once again marveled at the raw beauty of this wild coastline. A few fishing villages sprinkled along the shore interspersed with the white water rivers rushing into the sea between rugged mountains with their feet in the surf.

There was one boat tied up to the inside of the T dock and three men were standing next to it watching me deplane. I knew the tall fit-looking one would be Rolf and the smaller and older man with the wild hair would no doubt be Rolf's friend and gun bearer, Moresby. The other man had to be the Client. Dressed in what appeared to be a spanking new Eddie Bauer outfit, he was a big man in every direction. My first thought was — how is this guy going to walk the 12 kilometers to the base camp? That's seven and a half miles! I slung my own backpack with my gear over my shoulder and walked to the boat as the seaplane revved the engine and pulled away from the dock heading out into the bay for his trip home.

Rolf and Moresby greeted me pleasantly and shook my hand. The Client stared at me, then turned to step onto the boat without a word. Rolf rolled his eyes and followed the Client aboard but Moresby helped me climb aboard, taking my backpack from my outstretched arm. He made a sudden movement as though he were dropping the backpack and I panicked. I cared nothing about the few items of personal clothing but the pack also had my camera gear and a brand new 600 mm lens, all loosely packed because we had to carry in and hardcases would not be easy to carry. The long lens was new to me because I had no interest in getting up close and personal with any of the ursine denizens of this back country. Moresby looked at me with a huge toothless grin, then burst out laughing. OKAAAY! A sense of humor even if it was at my expense.

    I helped slip the lines and the skipper of the boat smoothly headed out of the bay and made a right turn heading north. There was a fresh breeze out of the northwest as we cleared the headland and the quartering seas made us roll a bit but the big twin diesels put us crashing through the slight swell and we made good time northward bound. The Client sat on the aft cockpit bench with a can of beer and had yet to utter a word to me or anyone else. Strange fellow. If one was paying what I could only surmise was a huge fortune for this trophy bear hunt, one would expect some anticipation, a little excitement or at least a smile. But none of that showed as he just looked out to the passing shoreline off our starboard. Rolf and Moresby came out on the aft deck with coffee including one for me.

    "Ya, your pack, she is all you need? Not heavy. You bring little?"

    "Yup, only what I want to carry, like you said," as I smiled at Rolf.

Lesson Eighteen

"Sehr gut, sehr gut," he said, slapping me on the back.

At this point we were interrupted by the Client who was leaning way too far over the gunnel. Both of us jumped to grab his belt before he went overboard. We held him while he emptied his stomach and then offered him some coffee because his beer had spilled into the scuppers leaving a short telltale trail of foam indicating its exit.

By the time we reached the shore at the mouth of a small river, he had emptied himself several more times and was sporting a light shade of green nicely matching his new Eddie Bauer camo jacket. We unloaded quickly and shoved the bow of the boat back off the sand and thanked the skipper for the ride. Starting off inland following the river, Rolf and Moresby had large packs weighing in at about 65-70 pounds. Mine was only around 45 pounds, even with the extra 22 pounds Moresby had loaded and tied to the top of my pack. This I was able to manage. The Nikon camera with the 40-100 mm zoom lens hanging from my neck was probably the most awkward part of my load. The Client had no pack at all and I hoped for his sake his new hiking boots had been broken in before today's little jaunt.

The trek, mostly following a well beaten trail along the river, was not particularly steep, but we were always walking uphill. I kept my eye out for wildlife and finally felt it would be okay to shoot color photos of the Client now that his former green tinge had migrated to a reddish hue. Rolf motioned me to come forward.

"Zee Client, he not happy. Hunt big game in Africa. You know Africa hunt? Many servants, table mit vine und hot meal. Not here. You not take his picture unless I tell you, please."

    I readily agreed and after another hour Rolf called a rest and we waited for the Client to catch up with us. He had fallen maybe 75 or 80 yards behind the three of us. We ate sandwiches and refilled our water canteens from the stream and set out again after about a 20-minute break. Rolf happily proclaiming we were almost half way there. Mr. Client grunted and immediately fell back a few more steps.

    By the time we reached the camp, even I was puffing. Camp consisted of a 15 x 20 foot one-room shack, one over/under bunk bed, one single bed and several cots folded up against an outside wall. A pot-bellied, flat-topped stove sat in the center, surrounded by half a dozen camp chairs with a water urn on a table against the other wall. No white tablecloths at this Hilton which, in fact, probably more closely resembled the Hanoi Hilton. The Client was even less happy when he realized the toilet was a hole in the ground behind the shack with two rails to grab on to while stooping. Rolf mentioned to be sure to shovel in a bit of the sand from the pile next to the hole when we were done. Another grunt.

    Early the next morning we were a half mile away from the camp on the side of a foothill looking down over the valley and the stream roughly 400 yards away. I, with my small tripod and big lens (looking more like a cannon than a camera) was off to

Lesson Eighteen

one side of the natural blind that a rock outcropping provided where the Client rested his rifle while he sighted down to the stream. Rolf and Moresby knelt behind him, both with binoculars to scan the surrounding valley. Moresby spotted them first. Two bears ambled out of the wooded area upstream and into the stream.

"Two- or three-year-olds," he said quietly to Rolf.

The Client swung his rifle toward the bears as did I with my camera. The long lens was amazing. It brought the bears close enough to clearly see their claws sink into the gravel beneath the crystal clear stream.

Rolf tapped the Client on his shoulder and said, "No shoot. Too small. Not big. Vee vait."

I had hunted with my father and my uncles and my cousins for all of my young life but never anything this grand. Rabbits, squirrels, pheasants, ducks and geese and white-tailed deer every early winter were our targets back on the farm. We hunted, and everything we shot ended up on our table. I was never a good shot and in spite of the many warnings about keeping both eyes open for game, I was always the last to bag my limit, often because I missed so many easy shots. Shooting something simply for display was never in my consciousness.

Here in this vast wilderness, I was a bit disturbed about shooting a magnificent animal for what I considered no good reason. Rolf had explained that some of the meat would be packed out with them but the skin and the head were the first concern because that was what the Client was paying for today.

Two days passed with a few bears, but no big ones. Then on our third day, our luck changed. A couple of hours of observing two smaller males had passed when Moresby again pointed to the wooded area.

"More bears."

"Two females," Rolf confirmed.

Then one more bear padded out of the woods.

"Yaaa!. Papa comes for zee lunch. Maybe zis is zee von vee see last trip?"

"No. this one even bigger. I think he is our best one," Moresby said, maintaining his view through his binoculars.

Mr. Client again swung his rifle toward the bears, still a far distance up stream.

"No, no. Vee vait till he comes down ze stream, get much closer."

I was snapping photos as the four bears seemed to ignore one another. They gradually worked their way down stream, drawing closer to us but not yet at the closest point to our overlook. I had just loaded the third roll into the long lens camera and was checking the eyepiece through the camera around my neck when Rolf pointed at the bears. The big one had chased off one of the earlier bears and was now leading the four downstream. Through my long lens they appeared compressed and bunched together, but when I looked through the other camera, they had to be 10 or 15 yards apart in the stream.

The Client continued to track the bears with his rifle as they neared our range.

"Yaa, zee second from zee right. He is zee von. You shoot him now."

I could clearly see the big male in my tripod-mounted big lens and he was obviously much larger than any of the others. I began snapping more photos. Both Rolf and Moresby placed their own rifles next to them as they continued to watch through the binoculars. Pulling my eye away from the long lens, I snapped a few of the three men as they prepared for the kill. When Rolf again told the Client to take the shot, I returned my eye to the long lens camera on the tripod. I was double-checking the focus with one eye when the first shot rang out. It was startling for me, but more so for the bears. All heads snapped up to look in our direction. I was right on the big one but he did not seem fazed by the shot.

"Zee shot, she miss. Shoot again."

Another shot rang out and as I watched in my viewfinder, the big bear started walking in our direction. The other bears stood still in the stream staring up toward us.

"A miss. You must shoot again. Aim carefully," Rolf quietly encouraged the Client, who was now looking a bit flustered.

"Scope must be out of calibration. Thought you said you sighted it in," he yelled at Rolf. Those were the first words I had heard out of his mouth since I arrived.

"Zee gun, she is sighted correct," Rolf said under his breath. Then louder, "Squeeze, not jerk trigger."

"I know what I'm doing!" the client yelled back at him.

BANG, again. The bear was now running toward us and not slowing down. I watched this huge animal grow larger in my viewfinder as I continued to snap away.

"Vun more or I vill have to shoot," Rolf said, sounding irritated.

When the fourth shot rang out, the bear was in full gallop towards us. Covering huge chunks of land with each lunge, he continued to fill my viewfinder as I snapped shot after shot. At one point, he was so large in the viewfinder only his head and shoulder were in the shot. A second later, I could clearly see his large and sharp teeth as he charged uphill toward us. I suddenly realized this huge angry monster was nearly on top of us! I panicked. Jumping up from behind my camera, I turned to run when another shot rang out. I was already 10 feet away with my back to the men when I heard Moresby say, "Yes, he is down. Good shot."

I stopped and turned around. The bear was down but where was he? Then I realized an embarrassing truth. The bear, large as he was, was still a good two hundred yards away from our natural blind. Chagrined as I was, no one brought up my flight in the heat of those adrenalin-fueled moments. Rolf had shot the bear after four misses by Mr. Client who steadfastly claimed the gun was at fault. The next morning while Moresby and I fished for our lunch, Rolf sidled up next to me.

Lesson Eighteen

"Zee camera, she is like zee gun, no? You must keep both zee eyes open, I zink! Only zen you zee everyzing, ya?" Then he looked me in the eye and chuckled. Damn, those were Pa's words precisely, I thought to myself. I smiled shyly back at Rolf while my face turned a crimson shade of red.

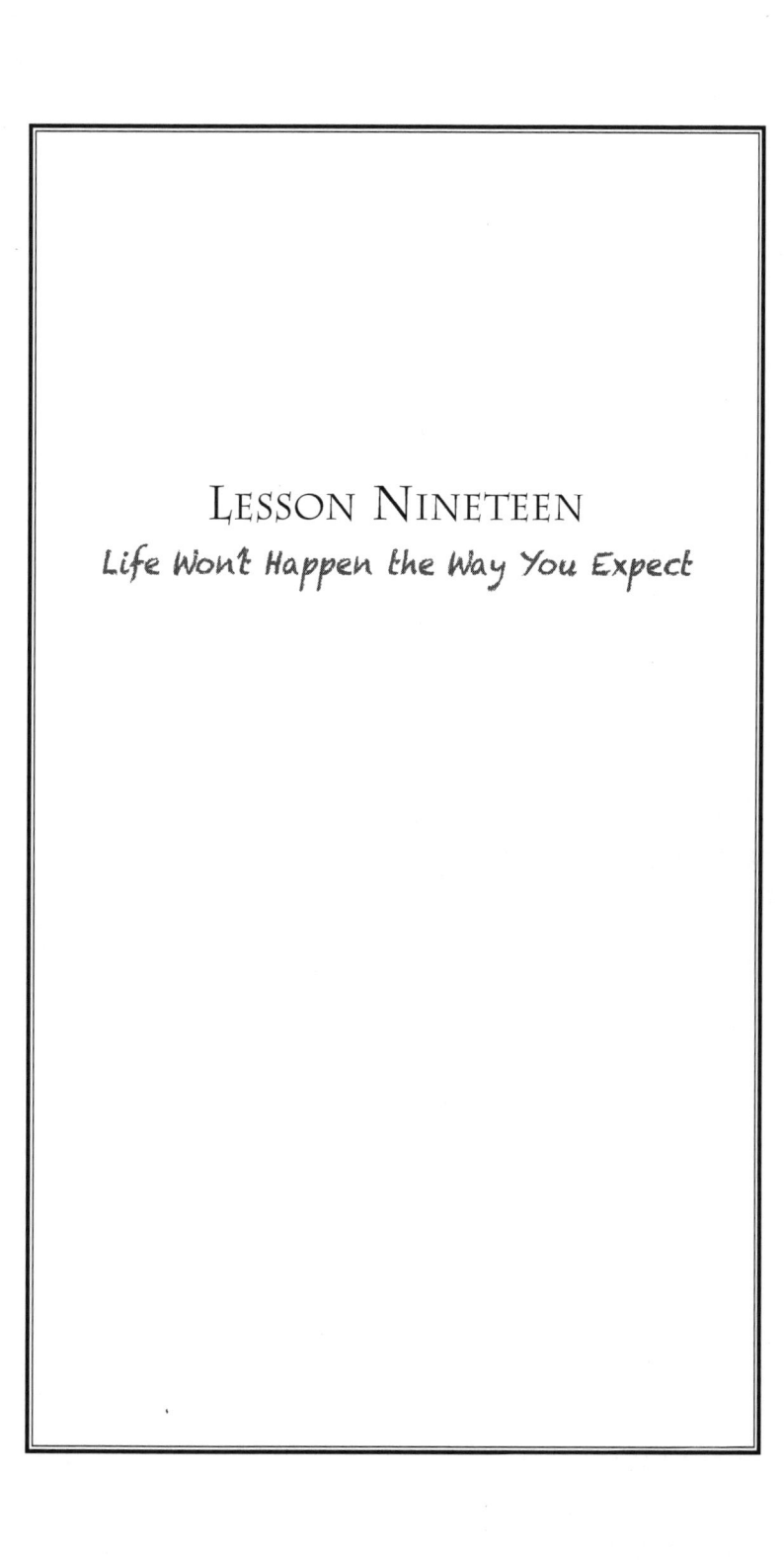

Lesson Nineteen
Life Won't Happen the Way You Expect

At least I wasn't shaking from fright this time

Moose-Taken Identity

B<small>Y</small> THE TIME I had reached my late teens, I felt confident that I knew everything of importance relating to manhood. I had purposefully chosen wilderness as my proving ground for two reasons. First, it was romantic to believe surviving off grid was an easily accomplished goal regardless of the voluminous amount of material claiming otherwise, and secondly, I was still afraid of the dark. What better way to prove my manhood more effectively than overcoming this character flaw in a dark and foreboding forest landscape? After a few years of increasingly isolated solo camping excursions I was feeling downright competent. I knew which items of equipment worked and which were ad-hyped junk. I was thoughtful and careful, I had expanded my competency, experience and confidence through trial and error while attempting to learn from every setback. Yes, there were many "learning moments," like realizing too late that even a small black bear can tear open a tightly sealed aluminum cooler I used to store a hefty slab of bacon. Now, however, about to leave my teens in the rearview mirror, I felt competent in most any woodsy milieu. I knew what to expect.

    Hubris does not announce its arrival with a trumpet. It quietly sidles up beside us and whispers in our ear only the words we wish to hear. Men who have spent their lives under the wide-open skies of wilderness know too well the dangers of thinking their personal world is under their own control. That form of hubris has damaged bodies and ended lives. Yet that sober realization is often hidden from us by said hubris.

One of Pa's muttered comments under his breath when he thought no one was within earshot was a simple, "Darn, never happens the way it should." At times it would be a louder expressed frustration, "Stuff just never happens the way I expect." Because I heard it almost exclusively in our basement workshop, I naturally assumed this frustration and outburst was project related. In my defense, I need only point out that humans learn via the same method we use to train our pets. Repetition. Blinders firmly in place, I moved through my teens oblivious to life's unexpected turns as anything more than my simple failure to correctly assess and predict those gentle swerves.

I had been offered an exciting opportunity to do a nature photography project during late fall in a Pacific coastal region of Alaska. It was a relatively simple request to photograph moose browsing in a swampy area as winter approached. The idea was to capture frost, steamy breaths and winter coats on these statuesque animals before real winter set in and photography would become far more difficult. The pay was nearly nothing, but I had been in the general area previously, so I knew the topography to a certain degree and besides, I wanted to do it! All I had to do was establish a blind at the most picturesque location,

Lesson Nineteen

plant a salt lick and wait. I estimated only a few days on site would produce plenty of opportunities for great photos. From a previous visit I knew there were moose in the vicinity, so I was pumped for the chance to use some new camera equipment and to get out into the fresh fall air again.

I made an arrangement to stay in a trapper cabin I knew of located a couple of miles off an old unused logging road that was another half mile from the swampy end of a small lake that I thought would be a perfect site. I spent the better part of the day packing in enough nonperishable staples for a week's stay at the cabin, although I did not expect to be there that long. The most unwieldy item was a thirty-pound block of salt I would use as a lure to keep my subject occupied while I snapped away, recording him for posterity. Later the same afternoon I hiked over to the area I thought most promising and sat down on a stump to think about what would work after I found what I took to be a well-used game trail with recent moose tracks.

The weather was perfect — a slight breeze out of the north bringing the promise of chillier air, keeping the few bugs still around at bay. The wind direction was consistent this time of year and so I set the salt lick in a rotting stump upwind of my camera blind but smack in the middle of the game trail. Assuming any moose would approach from lakeside, I did not want him sensing me if he was downwind. He may not have the greatest eyesight but he would readily smell me half a mile away if I were upwind of him because my scent would carry a long, long way on any light breeze. The block of white salt would not be visible from my camera position but easily available to Mr. Moose.

      Once I had located the salt lick position, I had to find the best camera location to install my blind. I had to be far enough away to remain hidden, yet close enough so I could avoid using a long telephoto lens and its telltale "compression" factor that I found so objectionable in many wildlife photos. Locating just the right distance, I then sighted to the salt lick and noted which branches and bushes hindered a clear view. Using a small machete, I carefully trimmed the offending branches without making it look as though I had chopped a tunnel to my subject. Satisfied with my view, I scooped out a shallow ditch long enough for me to stretch out on my belly and laid a plastic liner down. I assembled my 20 inch high camo tent/blind over the trench and walked a few yards in every direction to survey my handiwork. Satisfied that I would be reasonably well hidden from any moose visiting the saltlick, I hiked back to the cabin to turn in early because I had to be up before daylight and ensconced in my hidey-hole, cameras at the ready when the sun came up. I did not really expect any visitors on the first day but had high hopes for the second day. Moose tracks around the edge of the lake were fresh and I would guess the salt lick would not remain undiscovered for long. Were it earlier in the fall, I would have been more concerned about bears, but I was reasonably sure they were already lying

Lesson Nineteen

down and living off the layers of fat they had put on during spring and summer foraging.

Later that night, the cold front I had tasted on the wind the day before slid into the valley on a freshening breeze. The hike in the dark to the blind was more time consuming as I stumbled around, cursing the cloud cover that deprived me of moonlight, but I was able to crawl in before daybreak and then settled in for a quiet wait. It was not all that quiet with the wind gradually increasing and rattling the remaining leaves and bare branches, but I neither saw nor heard anything else except wind noise and swishing tree branches.

Day two on moose watch was identical to day one, except a few degrees colder. Nothing approached my tasty salt block. I had hoped this might be the day but I was sure it would now be tomorrow. Tomorrow, however, was not to be my day either, except for one surprising moment. Late morning, a Bald Eagle alit on the salt stump with a squirrel firmly in its talons. He did me a huge favor by flying off without strewing picked over bones and chunks of fur all over the salt lick. But no moose. I was beginning to think I may have chosen the wrong tactics or even the wrong location. It seemed perfect . . . a little standing water still covered with some green watercress-like plants, some still green bushes around the perimeter — what more could a foraging moose want? Tomorrow, day four, I would search out more tracks and consider relocating the whole operation. I fell asleep visualizing moose and dreamt of two bulls fighting over my salt block.

When my alarm went off in the dark, I sensed something different. It was downright cold. In fact, nearly freezing in the cabin. Immediately building a small fire to heat some water for coffee, I realized I had been a bit neglectful. The water carrier I had filled at the stream when I was hiking in was nearly empty. Thank the gods there was enough for today's coffee supply. Packing a pocketful of jerky and nuts, I headed out to the blind. I hadn't expected it nor was this cold predicted. Luckily for me I had a warm thermos and several hand warmers. I would be fine.

There was hoar frost on everything and if we got any early morning sunshine, that same everything would be brilliantly adorned in diamond-like glints that would make spectacular photos. I suddenly had a really, really good feeling about day four. The one sour note was the crunch under my boots. The ground was rapidly freezing. I would have a devil of a time trying to move the blind now. Maybe I would wait and see if the day brought me some good luck. Meaning a real live moose.

I did not get any rays of sunshine so my diamond sparkling forest never materialized, but a moose did. I caught a glimpse of a cow moving away from the target spot but the underbrush in that direction was too thick and I could not even tell if she had a young one with her. Worse, the wind was causing so much racket I could not discern specific sounds from any direction. Disappointing for sure, but perhaps progress in baby steps! Outside of the half dozen shots of the eagle resting on the stump, I had not shot

Lesson Nineteen

a complete roll of Kodachrome film yet. I left the blind early knowing I had to get water from the stream so I'd be able to heat up some soup for tonight and have hot coffee tomorrow. I would not mind if the weather warmed up a bit either.

I woke up once during the night and a howling wind whistling through the trees seriously dampened my spirits. If the wind held, every living thing within twenty miles of this little valley would be hunkering down for the day. When the alarm woke me a few hours later, the first thing I noticed was the silence. No wind, no rattling tree branches, no sounds at all. With revived hopes for the day, I prepped for the expected cold and set out. As I opened the door, I thought I had overslept. Bright as midday, the moon shone down on a brilliant blue-white landscape. Snow! And still drifting down in light flakes. Wow, now I was sure the gods were making up for the entire frustrating week. Of course Mr. Moose would make his appearance today! I was sure of it. The stars were aligned!

I crawled into my cozy little blind, wrapping the sleeping bag around me firmly, and waited for the dawn while sipping my coffee. Perhaps the sense of relief from the wind dying, or the fact that I had not slept well worrying about the wind let me doze off with my forehead resting on the back of my ice-cold Nikon. A soft, but decidedly strange sound woke me from my reveries. A snuffling sound. Muted but distinct. It moved closer to me from behind as I tried to wake up and identify where I was and what I was doing. The snuffle became louder as I peered out of the front of my blind. It was only a 15- by 15-inch opening so I could see very little to either side. Slowly and carefully, I stuck my head out just a couple of inches and twisted my neck in the direction of the strange sound. I was not going to make any sudden moves and scare away any game near me. I wanted to use up some of those rolls of Kodachrome 36 exposure film!

    What I saw froze me in place. Just next to me and standing 10 feet above was a huge bull moose snorting and snuffling as he looked straight ahead. A full-grown moose can weigh over 2000 pounds! With huge wide feet/hoofs that they put to excellent use in soft and swampy ground or the body parts of a marauding wolf, even bears are reluctant to take them on. And this one was standing practically on top of me! How could he not smell me? Then I realized a slight breeze had come up from behind me while I slept and was carrying my spoor away from him and me and toward the salt lick. An unfortunate warmth spread throughout my midsection, bringing with it a characteristic aroma, yet I could not move. I was frozen in place but not from the cold. No, sheer terror coursed throughout my veins and froze me into a solid block of inaction.

    The bull moose, totally oblivious to me directly beneath him, quietly plodded off toward the salt lick. If he sensed me when he got downwind of me, he gave no indication of it, but I am sure the smells he was getting now would be a mixed bag. He ambled

Lesson Nineteen

over to the salt block and took a few licks. Then he stood tall again and looked back at me. To say I had recovered my composure would be a lie. My hands were shaking as I tried to focus the new Nikon camera I had knocked off the small tripod stand in those first few post-trauma seconds. Pushing the shutter release button produced zero results because while I had dozed, a few flakes of snow had settled on it and it was half frozen.

By the time I got the camera off the little tripod, cleaned the lens and dusted the snow off the shutter release, a full minute or two had passed. Mr. Moose was not about to wait around for me to act like a professional, the result being I got only a few shots of him looking back at me with what I am convinced was a snarky smile. I do know I was still shaking, because weeks later when I saw the slides, all my Mr. Moose shots were out of focus. Thinking that all my far-sighted preparations would cover any and all probabilities and produce a successful result no matter what was the epitome of hubris. Pa was right . . . again. Life never happens the way you expect. I did get a couple of decent Bald Eagle slides however.

Lesson Twenty
Good Deeds DO Go Unpunished

Narrow forest roads are dangerous at night viewed through tears

My Momentous Midnight Ride

My FATHER CAN DO anything in the whole world, except one. My father cannot speak to me on the telephone. I've never determined exactly what chromosome is missing in his DNA string to preclude him from speaking to me on the telephone, I just know it IS missing and he doesn't. It's not that my father isn't interested in what's going on in my life I'm sure, because during my mother's calls I can hear him in the background constantly prompting her with questions and corrections throughout the entire conversation. Sometimes, when I hear that disembodied background voice, I visualize a talking 55-gallon drum, fiber optic network notwithstanding. So late one Wednesday afternoon, when my secretary poked her head in the door and told me my mother was on the line it struck me as neither strange nor out of the ordinary. I put down my pen, picked up the phone, and leaned back expecting to hear the latest gossip from the Great Northwoods, where my folks had retired less than a year before.

    But my Mother's voice DID sound out of the ordinary. It was furtive, hushed, and she obviously wanted to be done with the call posthaste. This was unlike my Mother, who will routinely carry on long personal conversations with strangers in the checkout line at any given grocery store. Now however, she wanted to end the conversation and get off the phone as quickly as she could. It took me a few moments to grasp the meaning of her words, and when I did, it was somewhat unnerving.

By a series of coincidences, I had not seen my folks in the flesh for about six months. I had talked to them (I mean to my mother, of course) at least once a week, but we were never able to coordinate schedules, what with her visiting relatives and me traveling for business. So when she explained how difficult a time my father was having adjusting to retirement, it was impossible for me to visualize the reality of her spoken words or their seriousness. What could she mean? They were at the beginning of their planned great adventure, that of a long and deserved retirement. Many nights had I passed at the kitchen table with them as they planned strategies and poured over retirement lake house brochures. I suppose, upon reflection, it would not be unlike many other hard working men of my father's generation, who, retiring early, sensed a lack of purpose in their lives after careers had prematurely turned the corner into history.

Although just 50, my own father had completed a quarter century of exciting and satisfying service as a fireman in the department of a major city. His career had been a glorious time for me. Still a time for heroes, my friends and I willingly looked for role models and firemen were always at or near the top of our list. My father, however, was in a class by himself. He loved his job for more than it was, cared about it passionately, earned a slew of commendations along with a fat scrapbook filled with news articles and photos of himself carrying assorted men, women, and children out of burning buildings. All lovingly collected and annotated by my mother, and ogled over at every opportunity by me and my younger brother. My father, of course, thought it all nonsense and refused to look at the book, but even he could not deny the truth of his accomplishments nor his bravery as recounted in yellowing newsprint and flashbulb lit 8 by 10 glossies.

Growing up in that household was both exciting and difficult for my kid brother and myself because there literally was nothing our father could not or did not know how to accomplish. Build a garage, save lives, hang drapes, cook, coach boxing, or catch fish when every one else came home with empty creels was simply a natural occurrence for him. He never talked about doing a difficult job, he simply did it. My brother and I learned by osmosis as best we could, but knew we might never reach his levels of competency. And because of this god-like quality, any questioning, disapproving or — heaven forbid — disagreeing with him, was well beyond our ken.

Not that my brother and I were angels of any sort, far from it in fact. We went to extraordinary lengths to ensure that any actions of ours that might incur parental wrath would only come to light on those days that our father would be at the firehouse. In those days, a typical work rotation for a fireman was 24 hours on duty and 24 hours off. This meant we could count on a full 12 hours of cooling off time before Pa got home. In spite of this brilliant strategy, we often spent sleepless nights worrying about his early morning homecoming, and how much wrath would carry over with his arrival. Our house was filled by him, and we never questioned his all encompassing presence whether he was there in body or in spirit.

Today, strangely enough, although my brother and I are totally different people, with values as far apart as one could imagine, and the wide gap between us bridged only by arguments, there remains one single unshakable bond uniting us. We both see this man bathed in the same glowing light. We both worship the ground he walked on and will continue to do so to the end of our days. We might do so for different reasons, but it is worship nevertheless. Our "father/hero" stories have bored friends for years, yet neither one of us seems to have suffered any of the angst or bitterness one hears about in families with strong, overpowering father images. I know for a fact that we both felt incredibly lucky to have this man to look up to.

Could this person now being described by my mother actually be the same man? My father, moping around the house, not eating, refusing to go out, seemingly intent on wasting away to dust, waiting for the last fire bell? Hardly! After all the years of planning by the two of them, doing exactly what he was now doing? Retired at an early age with a beautiful home (built entirely by you know who) on a small spit of land extending out into one of the most fruitful fishing lakes in the heart of God's North Country. I quickly grasped the irony of it all and laughed. BZZZZT . . . wrong response. The mere tone of her voice severely chastised me. My Mother was worried . . . seriously worried.

"He never smiles anymore," my mother went on . . .

Well, I never remembered him as a smiling kind of guy, anyway. His Teutonic demeanor was always serious. We all knew it didn't mean he was unhappy, it simply meant he was living out his ethnic heritage.

"He's lost twenty pounds and his skin is pasty pale. He won't even mow the grass," she related to me.

This news was more disturbing. My father is a huge bear of a man who has always needed to keep busy doing one project or another. He can't help it. I have vivid memories of our manicured lawn, whether done by his own hand or by me and my brother under his close and constant tutelage (it had to be constant). A shaggy lawn was definitely out of character for the man.

"Is he sick?" I asked her, "Have you seen the doctor?" Knowing full well what her answer would be, it chilled me nevertheless.

"No," she said, "You know him. He won't go. It's as though he's waiting to die."

How could this be, this man, this superman, barely fifty years old, thinking about death?

"I'm worried sick," she went on, "He needs something more in his life. He needs to go back to work. He needs a job. You're the oldest. You have to do something, you have to tell him," she implored, "and I mean right now."

"Me? Me? You want ME to do something? Do what?" I asked incredulously. What could I possibly do or say to my father? His wishes and ways were to be emulated and copied, not questioned! In my entire life I never talked back to my father nor did my brother. Talking back to the man was something you didn't do. We believed death to be the logical result if we had, even though I cannot remember one instance of corporal punishment in all of my childhood. I don't think my brother would be able to think of any either, and still, we had this fear, this respect, this image of a Being so omnipotent he was unassailable. And now my mother was asking me, no — telling me — to drive 400 miles, get out of the car, walk up to my father and calmly mention to him to get a life, because he was screwing up this one. It would be as though I, an inferior clone, was personally passing judgment on his choices, his worth — his life. I could not imagine the magnitude of the earthquake that would rumble out from that epicenter of their small kitchen were I to dare tell my father what to do with his life. "Hey Pa, get off your butt and get a job," would have been laughable if it had not been so implausible. It could certainly be his line, but never mine, not even in my thoughts. It was unthinkable and I told my mother so in loving but pleading terms. "Don't make me do this," my mind silently screamed out to her, while my calm executive voice iterated all the practical reasons why such tactics would not work with this man.

Lesson Twenty

To no avail. One's mother is not a woman to say no to under any circumstances. It was the quintessential rock and a hard place. I could not say no to my mother's request, and I could not say those harsh words to my father. I dealt with the two opposing dilemmas the same way most of us do, passing on the first, while hoping the second would dissolve before any action became necessary. I told my secretary I would be leaving early and probably would be gone the rest of the week. With foreboding, for I could see no sane resolution resulting from this craziness, I packed a few things and set off on the six hour drive to my parents' northern Wisconsin lake home.

Six hours of thought, trepidation and near panic. Who was I to do this foul thing? The elder son? The Ne'er-do-well? The admitted Black Sheep? Yes, all of those things, but more than any of them — loving son. Adoring son. Admiring son. And what could I expect in return . . . enmity of the man I revered? A tarnishing of my lifetime idol? Of course! And that was probably the best I could expect. Those six hours were not the luxurious hours cruising through the lush northern lakes country, insulated from the cares of the office that I normally would have looked forward to with relish.

I remember only snippets of our meeting. Brilliant tiny stars salting the midnight black sky as I eased the car down the quarter mile, tree-lined gravel driveway to their home. Headlights illuminating individual trees like a newsman's flashbulb, and then car and headlights both sucked into nothingness by the vast expanse of inky water lapping near their porch steps. The bare bulb over the porch flickering on, but unable to wrest more than a few feet from the overpowering dark. My father's shock at seeing me (my mother of course would not have told him of my coming or it's purpose). My shock at seeing him. The instant worry on his face that whatever the problem that had brought me to his door, it must be severe. My father, shrunken and pale just as my mother had described, standing on the stoop in his pajamas, yet fully prepared to charge into the fiery blaze once more for his son, who must have bad troubles to be here on his dark stoop at this even darker hour. The strong coffee moments later on the familiar red Formica kitchen table with the ridged metal edging that I kept picking at with my fingernails, just as I had done for twenty years growing up. But the words . . . oh yes, the words I recall with total clarity. The shockingly sudden and cold, quiet words: "No son of mine talks to me like this at my own table." And these crushingly final words were spoken softly, as he rose heavily, turning his back, walking away.

I do remember the six hours and 400 mile return home. Punctuated every 20 miles with a stop at the side of the road in futile attempts to wipe away first, my tears, then my ingratitude, and finally, my shame. I hid in the closet of my mind and refused to open the door to anyone. The only role that had meaning in my life was that of the good son. And now that had slipped silently away from me like the promise of my

Lesson Twenty

youth. My father's intoned words from those same years came back to me in a raging torrent.

"The only riches in life are family and friends," he would say whenever I would sit still long enough to be within earshot, "nothing, but nothing, is more important than family and friends. Never forget that."

I hadn't forgotten that. I hadn't forsaken those words. And I hadn't forsaken those ideals. But yet, in spite of remembering, the empty cold of that hot August month froze my whole being. Maybe "they" were right . . . no good deed goes unpunished.

Time meandered unimportantly. I don't remember how long it took for it to happen, but my mother's voice on the telephone was warm.

"He's found a job. He's working. You have to come home. He misses you."

My ice age had melted in the warmth of those few words. In the ensuing years, and there have been many, not one of us has ever mentioned my momentous midnight ride, but my mother smiles at me with her eyes. And I can't think of a nicer thing to have happen to me. Good deeds DO go unpunished. Of course, once in a while, one must be patient.

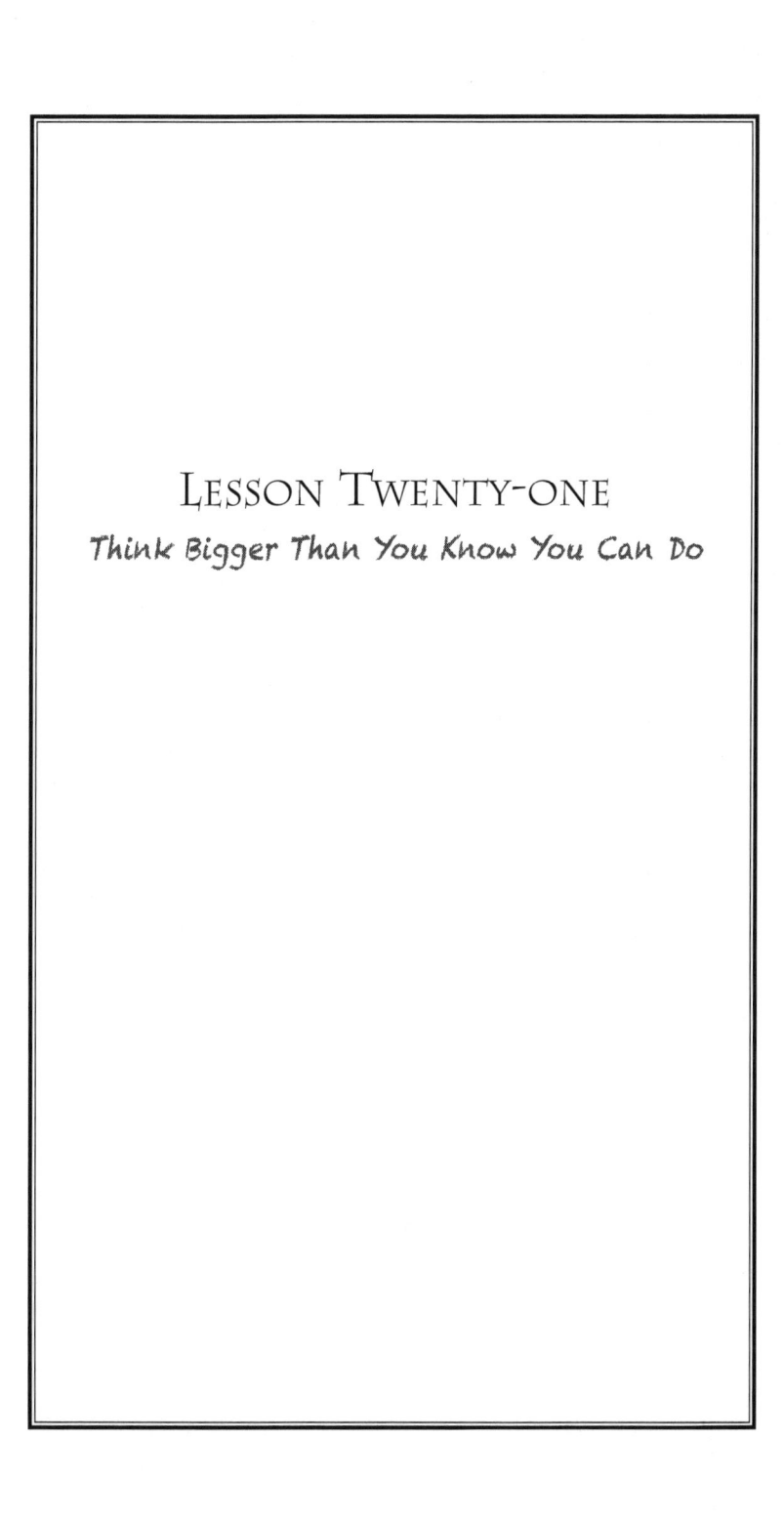

Lesson Twenty-one
Think Bigger Than You Know You Can Do

*Not only heavier than they appear,
but far more expensive as well*

Pleasing the Old Man

As I have often stated herein, my father is a hero. Oh, not just to me, but to a lot of people. He's got trophies from school teams, medals from the big war, and a large newspaper clipping file that my mother saved during the twenty-five years he spent as a fireman. So when I think of my father, a certain awe creeps into my consciousness. Don't misunderstand me, my father is the last one you would ever hear these things from. He'll go to his grave denying all of it and saying that he was only doing his job. But the facts and the saved lives are the indisputable truth of what I say. And that brings me to why I'm telling you this. I have always tried to please my old man. And what's more, he's always been pleased. But you know how it is when, in your heart, you know you'll never come up to the standards he's lived all of his life.

Now this is beginning to sound like one of those "poor me" stories, but it's not that way. My Pa was, is, and always will be the best Old Man a guy could ever hope for. And this is just one more little incident about his son who loves him with all his heart, but is somewhat of a ne'er-do-well and at 44 years of age didn't have a lot to show except a broken marriage, a good woman he didn't marry, mucho debt, and a whole slew of big ideas. One of those big ideas came up that summer when a good friend who works for our city government (she's actually a big wheel) came over with the news that our city was going to auction off the old "stand on the corner" fire alarm boxes. You know the kind, red square boxes with a little blue light on top and ugly blue stanchions on the bottom. They must weigh in at about half a ton. They have caused many a hernia in kids who have tried to tip them over (first hand experience). My friend said, "Wouldn't one of those look good on my patio decking? I could put a phone in it!" I said I thought it was a stupid *objet d'art* to put in a well designed wood deck patio. All the while, I was saying to myself, what a great piece of memorabilia for my father, the retired fireman. The more I thought about it, the more I knew this was an Old Man pleaser to beat them all.

     I began to formulate the plan. One always has to be careful when dealing with my Old Man, particularly if it involves giving him a gift that costs 50 or 75 bucks. As a policy, our family has never been big on gifts, so I had to make sure he didn't have the opportunity to say it cost too much. As I've noted, my folks live in Northern Wisconsin during the summer in a house my father built on a spit of land sticking out into one of the best walleye lakes in the whole country. In the morning you can sit at the kitchen table with a cup of coffee and watch the changing patterns on the water out of three sides of the house. The hummingbirds come up to the window to be fed and a local flock of ducks, who think my Pa is the Corn King of the North Woods, spend the entire summer on the porch. Now wouldn't that fire alarm box look great out there on the lawn between the two jackpines next to the water? Of course it would! Ah, but how to get it in place without the Old Man suspecting something. I mean, a present that is this spectacular just has to be a surprise, right?

Simplicity rules. Drive up 400 miles with the monster sticking out of the trunk and stop in town. Call one of the neighbors and ask them to get my folks out of the house for an hour while I drive over and set up the box in the yard next to the water where they'll see it the second they come home. Then, whammo, I reappear 20 minutes later dressed in the garb of the conquering hero. Magnificent. My folks will be dining out on this story for a whole winter in Florida. Also my Pa can spend every spring repainting that ugly thing. How could he not be pleased?

The Saturday of the auction is a hot and sticky 94 degrees. Great, I think to myself, nobody will show up in this kind of heat and maybe I'll get it even cheaper than I had planned. Maybe I'd have a few bucks left over to buy some of that paint to go with it, just to give the Old Man a head start, you understand. My friend, who by now thinks of the idea as hers, is with me and we have borrowed one of those little toy Japanese trucks to carry the two fire alarm boxes home.

The first inkling of a fly in the ointment is the traffic. We have to park at least three quarters of a mile away and walk to the grounds. Sweating profusely, we arrive only to find the line for a bid card is about as long as the walk from the car. Undaunted, we get in line, telling each other all these people are here for the hundreds of other items at auction. Fifty-five humid minutes later we get to the compound where the alarm boxes are being kept for inspection. It's hard to tell what they look like because the crowd milling around them is six deep. This is not the way I had envisioned the event.

It is an interesting crowd however. A great deal of polyester was populating the grounds and a lot of the guys were wearing hats that said "support your local fireman." It's a carnival atmosphere and everybody is slapping somebody on the back and shaking hands with that look that says, "Should I know you?" Well, I've known firemen all my life, and a tighter skin-flinty bunch you would be hard pressed to find, so even with the crowd I'm not too worried. But there sure are a lot of people here.

The auctioneer finally makes his way to the alarm boxes after we've spent another hour standing around sweating and he begins the bidding. Now, for me to come up with a hundred dollars cash money for this gift was no mean feat. I was proud of the fact that I hadn't spent it on something foolish like food or rent. I had looked these boxes over pretty carefully and knew they would start the bidding with the least desirable ones, so I decided to get mine early before they got to those that looked like they had never seen time in my neighborhood. Eighty of these behemoths standing next to one another is an impressive sight, overshadowed only by the four hundred people hovering over their individual favorites.

Lesson Twenty-one

The auctioneer took one look at this crowd and knew immediately that he had a goldmine about to be staked out. Sure enough, he opened the bidding at two hundred dollars and before I knew what had happened, it was gone at six hundred and fifty dollars. Serious trouble. Six hundred and fifty U.S. dollars? And this one was the wreck of the lot! I couldn't believe it. It also took my friend aback. Even with her steady job, I think the patio was looking better to her without the fire box/phone booth.

The gist of the matter is that we stayed all afternoon braving sunstroke hoping for a break. No luck. Six hundred and fifty was the cheapest, and they ranged all the way up to $1600. Both of us went home hot, sweaty, depressed, and wondering just what kind of nut would spend $1600 on a Model K 1928 "stand on the corner" fire alarm box? After all, they are very ugly.

What kind of nut indeed! I'll tell you what kind of nut! Pa . . . if I had had the $1600, you'd have a brightly polished Model K 1928 red and blue fire alarm box sitting right between those two big jackpines next to the water — right this very minute!

Lesson Twenty-two
You're Never Too Old to Listen

*Beaches in Normandy
extend seemingly forever at low tide*

Planning Ahead

BACK IN THE LATE SIXTIES, while I was busy being deceived by some government bosses, the subject of war came up with my father. When I was a child, my mother had shown me a box full of medals Pa received but would never talk about. And we'd always skipped over the postcards they had received from me with the Laotian and Cambodian postmarks, but I questioned him once about his Atlantic adventures early in the big war (twice torpedoed and once in the hospital for two months) and why he volunteered for the Navy Frogman program that was the precursor to the current Navy SEALs. He said he did it because they refused him for the submarine service. He then told me in two or three clipped sentences the only story about the war that I ever heard from him. He spent the two nights before D-Day underwater off Utah Beach assessing the anti-landing installations along the shore while a storm raged above him. This was just prior to the 25th anniversary of the Normandy Landings and I asked him if he intended to go back there. His reply was slow in coming, but he finally said what he always said about the war, "It was a bad time and not worth remembering or rehashing." I forgot about that conversation for a long, long time, until a year or two before he died when we once again got on the subject of the war and D-Day. He mentioned offhandedly that he may have made a mistake about never having gone back. Of the twenty men in his frogman unit he was the only one to survive the war. And he once again closed the subject and I promptly let the conversation wander elsewhere.

    In October of 2003 I surprised my friend Kristine with tickets for us to go to Paris and visit my former boat neighbor, now living in La Rochelle on the western coast of France. Kristine said "Good timing." She had some business in Caen up near Normandy and could we combine the two? I readily agreed and then, recalling the last conversation with my father about D-Day, I decided I would also like to go to Utah Beach and spread a bit of my father's ashes in the surf, thereby at least taking a small part of him back to the site he belatedly wished he would have revisited while he was alive. I am an incurable romantic and have been dropping a bit of Ma and Pa's ashes wherever I might travel these past few years simply because I no longer am able to write them the post cards they so enjoyed. I felt that in a small way perhaps they would be able to experience the places they only read about from my reports while they were alive. Corny, but then I'm a Midwestern farm boy and am into corn big time.

    We finished her filming business in Caen after lunch and took off on the twenty-mile drive to the D-Day beaches. What had started out a beautiful sunny day rapidly deteriorated as a low came in off the English Channel and a twenty-five knot wind accompanied by sheets of horizontal rain made my thin summer raingear poor protection against the cold and wet. Arriving at the Utah Beach Memorial, I parked the car and looked at Kris while the windshield wipers beat a losing battle with the wind and rain. I told her I was obligated to do this now that I was here but she was certainly welcome to stay in the car while I just popped over the large dune in front of us to spread the small vial of my father's ashes in the surf. She said no; my father was one of her favorite people and she wanted to be there when I returned a part of him to the sea. We bundled up as best we could and climbed the 30-foot sand dune hiding the shoreline from our view.

    Stepping up into the unfettered force of the wind and rain driving in off the Channel, I stared for a few moments at the shoreline. I couldn't believe my eyes. The shore was at least a half mile away through an oyster farm! Low tide at the end of October is very low and the actual shore looked to be a half mile upwind! I again looked at Kris and she said, "Hey, we're already wet . . . " and so we began slogging through the muddy sand, our heads bent low to avoid the stinging pellets of raindrops. By the time we reached the actual shoreline both of us were soaked and our teeth wildly chattering from the cold.

    But I was here at Utah Beach, the site of one of my father's memorable life adventures, and so I carefully pulled out the little vial of ashes from my now sodden coat and bent over the water. I know I get maudlin about times like this, but I felt I was doing something my father would have approved of and liked. "Well, Pa, you're finally back here," I thought to myself. I removed the cap, turned the vial upside down, and a perverse gust blew most of his ashes over my face and up into the turbulent clouds. More than a few tears welled up uncontrollably. It was at this very moment that I heard several smothered guffaws from directly behind me.

    I stood up and turned around to see Kris making a woefully ineffective attempt to stifle her laughter. I looked at her and asked what was so funny about what I had thought to be a solemn moment. She said through small outbreaks of laughter, "Here we are, soaked to the skin, teeth chattering from the cold, half a mile from the Memorial and I just know your father is up there somewhere laughing his butt off. He's shaking his head and laughing because his elder son, the longtime and quite experienced racing and cruising sailor in the family, never bothered to check the tide tables. And now I can just hear your father's words: 'Hey, it's raining and it's cold, so dump the stuff on the sand and get back in the warm car for pity's sake.' Yeah, he would definitely be finding this whole episode pretty hilarious, I think."

    I stared at her for a moment and then burst out laughing myself. She was absolutely right. My father would have known the weather and the high tide mark before he ever got to the parking lot. I, of course, never gave it a thought. Now into my sixth decade and the Old Man is still reminding me to listen. Kris and I stayed warm on the half mile trek

Lesson Twenty-two

back to the car by laughing and reminiscing about Pa and looking up into the sky. It might have been the wind or perhaps a bird, but once or twice I thought I heard a muffled guffaw from somewhere up there.

Epilogue

*An errant ray of sunshine lights up the far shore
in Pa's favorite view*

I ROLL SLOWLY DOWN the long sloping driveway at eleven in the morning, park the car in its usual spot, and walk the remaining twenty yards to my parents' Ramiroto lake house amidst the raucous swish and swirl of fallen leaves. The wind causes the rustling, moving carpet of dark red oak, orange-red maple, and bright yellow birch leaves to hide my tentative steps, obscuring the still green October grass beneath my feet. My steps are tentative because I'm back here to carry out a promise to my late father. He asked to have his ashes spread into the water just off the shore of his retirement lake home here in Northern Wisconsin. Unfortunately, I think to myself, today's wind is blowing strong out of the west and will probably send his ashes all the way to Michigan, a hundred miles away, rather than the few yards into his favorite walleye fishing hole. But first things first, and I need to talk to my brother, who has been up here with Mom this past week waiting for me to return.

I intend to close up the lake house and take Mom south to Milwaukee for the winter, but neither my brother nor I have ever closed up this house. That chore was the sole responsibility of my father for the 28 falls he and my mother left for Florida to escape the bitter cold and snow of the North Country. Now my brother and I must figure out the intricacies of draining all the water pipes, and clearing the toilet, sink drains and water traps so they will not freeze and burst during the long unheated winter. To determine which electrical circuits to turn off and where to store the myriad of tools used during the season is a little like trying to read Pa's mind, and both of us feel uncomfortable as we make guesses as to how best to duplicate the procedures Pa had developed and refined over the nearly three decades he and my mother spent in retirement here on Ramiroto Point.

    Perhaps it does take us longer than we had expected, and perhaps it's our mutual reluctance to face the sad task of our duty to Pa, but the inevitable end to our closing deliberations comes, and the two of us climb the basement stairs back into the kitchen where Ma has been patiently waiting for us to finish our talk. She has been waiting since July for this moment of closure. I can distinctly recall back in July, immediately after Pa's death, telling both my brother and my mother that I thought it best to do the spreading of ashes later in the year when the painful open wound of his passing had healed a bit and we could do it more as a celebration of all the pleasant life memories he left with us. I was kidding myself. It's not going to be any easier now than it would have been then. I believe now that my mother knew, but acquiesced to me because at the time I was not dealing well with Pa's passing.

Epilogue

My mother puts on her walking jacket to protect her from the biting wind, I take down the surprisingly heavy urn from Pa's closet, and we three walk down the steps and out to the point. We walk slowly because Ma, at 83, is a little unsure of her balance on the uneven ground, but mostly, we walk slowly because this is a painful goodbye for all three of us. The wind, as if sensing our sadness, has died completely and the mottled gray sky that had boiled across the horizon earlier has frozen in place. An eerie stillness has settled the water and our lake is more than quiet, it is mirror-like in anticipation of our approach. A mile away, across the lake, the pencil thin trees have kept only their very topmost foliage, giving the appearance of a thousand paint brushes, dull with dry yellow paint, standing each on end.

Ma leans against a paper white birch grown tall and strong at the very end of her land. On its lake facing side, this birch still bears the faint teeth marks of a long ago beaver attack, but no indication of why he decided to let it stand. My brother stands next to Ma, just in front of the 25 foot tall jack pine Pa and I had planted the summer my son, his first grandson, was born. Many was the birthday my son, Kevin, stood against that tree to measure his growth against that of "his" tree. Now towering high above my brother, it stands sentinel while Tom shoves his hands deeper into his pockets and stares down into the clear cold water surrounding us. With the urn under my arm, I gingerly step from land to a large rock along the shore. The entire shoreline of Ramiroto Point is protected by hundreds of large rocks and boulders, each dug from the back forty, each lifted with great effort into an old wheelbarrow, each placed strategically along the shore to ward off the effects of erosion on this fragile finger of land jutting out into Nelson Lake. Each and every rock, dug, carried, and placed with loving care by my father over the thirty years he spent here.

    I have spent the ensuing months after Pa died musing often upon what I would say at this moment. My father was my hero and I dreaded his leaving. I felt I would never be able to measure up to his demonstrated manhood, but with a few well chosen words, I could at least pay homage to his splendid example. Deeply felt personal emotions are always the most difficult to translate into words. I slaved. I sweated. I reworked the phrases, rewrote paragraphs, and selected each word as carefully as he had selected those rocks lining the shore. And now as I carefully remove the urn's cover and hand it to Tom, tears fill my eyes and my throat tightens, closes, preventing any words at all from escaping my lips. I look back to Tom and to Ma for inspiration but find only the same watery, glassy reflection in their eyes that cloud my own. I open my mouth to at least try mumbling a few words of my painstakingly memorized eulogy, but only silence emerges. Words no longer are important. I slowly tilt the urn and sift a portion of Pa's ashes onto the mirrored surface of the waiting water. The white cloud of my father's remains spreads swiftly, silently through the still water in an ever broadening

Epilogue

pattern, as if seeking to inhabit the very soul of his lake. I rise up, cross back to where Ma and Tom stand and we hug each other without speaking. Arms around each other, we three face the lake once more and look out across the wide expanse of quiet water. For a few brief startling moments, an errant ray of sunshine illuminates the treetops on the far shore, igniting them as a single line of blazing yellow torches etched against the steel gray horizon. And we three know the truth. Pa is finally back home . . . to stay.

Biographical Note

Roger Kay harbors a distinct hatred for cell phones, but in his defense, he is a life-long aficionado of indolence. He dithers interminably over careers past as business entrepreneur, motion picture director, boat bum extraordinaire, and sometime wordsmith. Now in his fifth childhood, he divides his time between AURORA, his trusty old trawler (currently lying at anchor in Tarpon Springs, Florida) and a dirt home on the shores of Lake Michigan in Milwaukee, Wisconsin.

Acknowledgements

I wish to thank all my friends, semi-friends and non-friends who have painfully listened to these stories over and over again for so many years and never stopped me. Thanks to my longtime editor and designer Nick Allez, who consistently finds errors to correct even when I do not think they are errors.

Special thanks to Chuck, Tom, Lili, Eddy and Linda for reading and encouraging me to finish it. No amount of thank-you's can repay my life partner Kristine for her perverse compassion in tolerating my idiosyncratic tendencies. You have always made me a better human being. Thank you.